The Horse Girl

Beverli Rhodes, after varied careers over decades in medical business analysis, catering, counter-terrorism resilience and infrastructure, has finally found the inner strength to write her second book. Her first, *Finding Your Cosmic Connection*, was published by Chameleon Press in 1990 and has become 'rare', as few copies survive.

She appears frequently on radio and television as an authority on PTSD and victimology, from a survivor's point of view. She is the founder of the Survivors' Coalition Foundation assisting survivors of traumatic events. She has lectured and appeared at many prestigious venues, including the Sun City Superbowl in South Africa.

Beverli was born in England in the 1960s. She lives with her partner in rural Kent, the 'Garden of England'.

Sharon Ward-Keeble has been an international journalist for more than two decades, specializing in articles about real-life people for a wide variety of newspapers and women's magazines in the UK and abroad. She has worked with Beverli Rhodes several times on articles about her childhood sexual abuse, coping with post-traumatic stress and how her horse gave her a new lease of life after she almost died in the London terrorist bombings of 7 July 2005.

An avid rider since childhood, she now owns four horses, two of which she regularly shows in dressage and show-jumping classes. She lives in Florida, America, with her husband and their three daughters, all of whom ride and appreciate the amazing bond that horses can form with their riders.

The
Horse
Girl

I survived abuse and a terrorist attack.
This is my story of hate, hope and healing.

Beverli Rhodes
with Sharon Ward-Keeble

JOHN BLAKE

Published by John Blake Publishing Ltd,
3 Bramber Court, 2 Bramber Road,
London W14 9PB, England

www.johnblakepublishing.co.uk
www.facebook.com/Johnblakepub ⓕ
twitter.com/johnblakepub ⓣ

First published in paperback in 2014

ISBN: 978-1-78219-918-2

British Library Cataloguing-in-Publication Data:
a catalogue record for this book is available from the British Library.

Design by www.envydesign.co.uk

Printed in Great Britain by CPI Group (UK) Ltd

3 5 7 9 10 8 6 4 2

Papers used by John Blake Publishing are natural, recyclable products made
from wood grown in sustainable forests. The manufacturing processes
conform to the environmental regulations of the country of origin.

Every attempt has been made to contact the relevant copyright-holders,
but some were unobtainable. We would be grateful if the
appropriate people could contact us.

I decided to move away from sweet silence; the haunting safety of saying nothing. I wasn't alone. My personal transformation would not have been possible without my human life partner and my furry four-legged partners. In writing this book, I likened it to placing a large artistic tattoo on one's face. I have to be totally committed, forever, accepting the reactions of friends, family and the readers, even if it is a string of criticism.

Thank you for being brave, helping me through the deep darkness, providing the sounds in the silence in the wilderness of my soul.

Thank you for giving and never asking, consoling me with the idea that there are no real devils in our world, only those running wild within our hearts.

This book is dedicated to all survivors, as a reminder to act. Forgiveness happens in an instant and is greater than any sacrifice. All that exists is not good or bad – it just is. Heal, in whatever way possible.

BEVERLI RHODES, May 2014

CONTENTS

CHAPTER ONE

LONDON TERRORIST BOMBINGS, 7 JULY 2005

It was the morning of 7 July 2005 and on that murky, damp, unseasonably cool day, I was in amazingly good spirits and excited for the working day to start.

I had a job working for one of London's top consultant firms, which I loved, even though the hours were long. The company were contracted to assist with winning London's bid for the 2012 Olympic Games. It was a private consultancy company in the City of London that had the contract for the bid and they worked along with officials of the City of London and the government. It was an incredible feat for the capital to win such a prestigious honour – a win that was actually several years in the making – and all of us at the firm had dedicated hundreds of hours to help ensure that our beloved country won the bid of a lifetime. When we finally did win the bid, it was absolutely thrilling because everyone on the close-knit

panel that had worked on the project knew that, with the words 'Olympic Games' in our portfolios, we could probably get a job in just about any other consultancy firm across the globe.

The night before, we had been celebrating our historical victory but the next morning, it was time to get on with the enormous job in hand and start organising for the Games. We all knew that it was never too early to start the preparations. I was already thinking about ways to make the Games safer. So we had think out of the box, find proven technology – for instance, to track health care, prescriptions, medical treatment, etc and link them with any special medical requirements of the athletes and other members of the Olympic family, to ensure their general welfare. Security was top of the agenda for that morning's meeting, with a specialist coming in from Switzerland to discuss the hard and soft ring, as well as to share the lessons learned from previous Olympic Games. Ironic really.

That morning, I had left the house I shared with my partner Tina in north London at around 6.30am. Tina was working in the health service at Barnett and Edgware Hospital, quite near to where we lived. She left for work around the same time as me – pretty much an average morning in our household, as it was in many Londoners' homes, I imagine.

'Have a nice day!' Tina said as she gave me a quick goodbye with a kiss on the cheek. 'You're going to have a busy one!' I was thoroughly prepared for another demanding day at the office and, actually, I couldn't wait to get to my desk so that I could really start to work on my future career.

I hopped on the Tube at King's Cross station at 8.42am and, up until that moment in my life, I don't think that I had ever been happier with my lot. My life felt pretty much mapped out and I liked the certainty. I was settled in a committed relationship with my delightful partner and we lived in a lovely house – a 1950s style two-story with a large bay window to the front and a fully paved driveway big enough to park a couple of cars.

We had a handful of good friends and a job I not only loved – even thrived on – but one that had made me proud to be British: it was the Olympic Games that had put the 'Great' back into Great Britain. I was looking forward to getting to the office at Lynton House in Tavistock Square, so I could meet with my colleagues and really get stuck into the job at hand.

As I stood on the platform at King's Cross Underground station, I looked around at everyone, as I always did. I loved 'people-watching' – it took away the boredom of waiting for the Tube train to arrive. I remember seeing people of all ages and backgrounds. And that morning there seemed a lot more of them than usual – the station was packed and, of course, the majority seemed to be getting on my train.

I snuggled into the crowded carriage. It was often a tight squeeze – so many commuters and never enough space. Somehow, I managed to grab a seat, where I sat clinging to my laptop and my bag full of Olympic Games info. This was one aspect of living in London that I confess I didn't like but was something, like so many other inconveniences, that I had to endure every day. The Tube is really the best

way to get around – it is the fastest and, generally, most reliable way of getting from A to B, so coping with this kind of difficulty, was simply what I regarded as one of the pitfalls of living in London and being able to enjoy all the city had to offer. And I have to say that, overall, I loved living in London. The vibrant cultural scene was intoxicating, I loved the diversity of the people who called the Capital city their home and, at the time, it seemed there had never been more of a sense of camaraderie – maybe, in part, because of the Olympic Games bid.

As the train approached Russell Square, I got up to make my way towards the doors. I knew from experience that, if I didn't get up from my seat early, the chances were I wouldn't make it through the sea of people, not only those already on the train, but also the ones who would be trying to get on once the train stopped and the doors opened. A couple of times in the past I had missed my stop because I'd left it too late to get up so, that morning, I had made sure not to repeat my mistake.

Then suddenly there was what I can only describe as a tiny sound, sudden and sharp, like the crunching of metal. At the same time, the train screeched to an abrupt halt. I was flung forward with great force. My face collided with one of the compartment's metal poles, and the next thing I knew I was lying on the floor and opening my eyes. I didn't know it at the time but I had been knocked out for 12½ minutes. For a few surreal seconds there was a complete silence on the train apart from the loud, high-pitched ringing in my ears, like when you come out of a nightclub and it takes ages for your ears to adjust after the loud noise.

I could barely see because there was smoke everywhere but, quickly, the silence was gone and I could hear people screaming and shouting, the panic in their voices reaching fever pitch. I don't know if anyone really knew what had happened but the first thing that came to my mind was that I'd been involved in a bombing. I had lived in South Africa for many years and guerrilla warfare permeated the way of life there. I knew what the sound of a bomb going off was like – it was a regular occurrence in South Africa, where guerrillas would set them off in buildings, by the side of the road, in packed market places – anywhere they knew that they would get the most casualties. And a bomb going off in London could only mean one thing – terrorists.

After the initial explosion the lighting had gone out and the dim emergency lights came on, like little specks of hope in the thick black smoke that filled the train. I could barely breathe, let alone see, so I felt my way along the floor towards where I thought the doors might be. I felt a warm, spongy feeling over my face and in my mouth – it was a very strange sensation and only later did I realise that blood was pouring from my face and mouth from where I had hit the metal pole. I clenched my teeth and I quickly realised that they were not where they should have been. I started to feel panicky as I felt around the inside of my mouth with my tongue. I only located my bottom set of teeth, which had been wedged by the force into my gums. They were wobbling all over the place and I somehow managed to squish them back into position. My chest was killing me and the whole left side of my face and body felt as if it was boiling, like really bad sunburn. At that time I

was completely unaware of my life-changing injuries – my one goal was to get the hell out of there, not that I even knew if it was going to be possible to do so.

The terrible screaming will live in my mind for ever. That horrific reality as people realised that something major had happened, that they were in great pain, or dying, or were just completely freaked out because it was so dark and so smoky. Most of those around me were struggling to breathe and were disorientated, as I was. We could have been plunged into the deep bowels of the earth for all we knew, never to see the light again. That's certainly what it felt like and I was under no illusions about the severity of the situation – that I might actually die on that train beneath London.

Like everyone else on the train who was still alive, I flipped open my mobile phone so that I at least had the faintest of light to assess what was happening around me. I heard my voice shouting, 'Don't panic!' and then someone else said the same thing. Something deep inside that was far stronger than me kept me calm and told me that I had to keep my wits about me, despite what I feared. Other voices were shouting, screaming – some for help and others, like me, trying to instil calm into the dozens of hysterical people who had got on the wrong train that day. I remember some stunned commuters didn't say a word, opting instead, I imagine, to pray to God for their lives in silence.

I took a woman's hand and we struggled to stand up. There was debris everywhere, as if the train had been literally mashed to a pulp. In the back of my mind, I knew

that many of the strangers around me were probably lying there dead. I imagined their relatives looking at their bodies and I hoped they were at least all in one piece. It's odd the things that go through your mind when you're in a crisis.

Through the smoke, I could vaguely see movements and I clung to those images. There was life inside of that carnage but, at first, that wasn't enough for me. I felt again that I was most likely going to die. At this point, I wasn't in much physical pain because I think that the adrenalin was fiercely kicking in, not allowing me to accept the situation and just lie down and die. There was so much blood – it felt warm and sticky on my fingers and it tasted metallic in my mouth. I could feel it dripping down my jaw and off my forehead.

In the midst of such destruction and horror, I found myself mentally doing what I can only describe as like a shopping list of my life so far and my emotions at the time. I thought about Tina and how I would never see her again. Had I told my daughters and Tina how much I loved them all? If not, why not? What if I might never again look out of my window and see the dreary London weather? What if I never got the chance to cuddle my dogs, or go back to work, or see my friends again? Was I truly destined to take my last breath that morning and, if so, was I leaving my loved ones in good positions, both financially and emotionally? The enormity of what dying really meant hit me in just a few seconds but, although I was heartbroken, I wasn't afraid of dying; I wasn't scared of passing over to a better life if it really was my time.

But as I staggered along that carriage and listened to my fellow passengers moaning for help, I knew that I owed it to myself to at least try to get off that train and seek help, even if it might prove futile. I had to try! I couldn't die without a fight – that would not have been me. The story of my life, really, has been a fight to survive and that's exactly what I did once again. I called on every bit of inner strength I possessed and decided that I was going to walk out of that tunnel and, if I was going to be OK, that would be a huge bonus. I didn't take anything for granted but I knew that I just had to try to save myself.

I called out to see who was awake – and who was alive. Someone had the idea to use the lights from our mobile phones to find the way out of the carriage. I later discovered that when the bomb had been set off in one of the carriages by suicide bomber Germaine Lindsay, an Islamic extremist, the whole train had gone into lockdown, so every door became jammed shut. I heard people say that there had been an electrical fault in the Underground and that had caused the explosion. Then someone else was screaming that the whole train was on fire and that the flames were heading for us. I still don't know how far our carriage was from where the bomb exploded but we could smell the fire's plumes and the smoke was like dense fog, so we knew that it was coming our way.

A young guy was determined to open the doors. I remember he was so adamant that he could break open those doors and get us all out of there. By the light of several mobile phones, he stuck his fingers in between the doors and he pulled and pulled with all the strength he

8

possessed. It was impossible – those heavy doors were not going to move. They weren't meant to move – this was an emergency and, at such a time, the doors are locked until someone outside the train can open them. At that moment, though, there was no one outside the train to rescue us. We were trapped inside a burning carriage and we all knew we had precious little time to get out of there before we were burnt alive. I later found out that the man in question had broken all his fingers trying to open those doors.

By sheer luck – I don't know what else to call it – the driver was still alive and he managed to open one of the doors at the end of the train that opens into another carriage. It was a tiny door with steps leading down onto the track. I guess that, even though we were in lockdown, that door was easier to open than the main sliding ones. That was going to be our escape route.

Some of the people who were on their feet were terrified that, if they jumped onto the train tracks, they would be electrocuted but the driver assured us that all power had been turned off, or had gone off with the explosion, which meant that it was safe to walk on the tracks.

Those of us who could still walk climbed down, the first one gingerly stepping onto the metal rails. That person was safe. One by one, we edged our way onto the tracks and then off to the side of them, feeling along the tiled walls of the tunnel. Outside the carriage the silence was eerie after the mayhem inside the train. The only sounds were those of steam escaping and the smashed-up metal moving around as it creaked to a resting place.

We were all black with soot and dazed with shock. I

think there were about a dozen of us. I remember feeling along the tiles because I couldn't see my own feet. It was horribly claustrophobic down there. Some of the tunnels are 30 metres below the surface, and we had only a tiny gap between the train and the wall, so that we were practically squashed like sardines as we passed through some parts of the tunnel. The odour was pungent – it smelled of piss and smoke and burning metal. Everyone was coughing and spitting, trying to find the will to keep going, as we slowly headed towards Russell Square station, with no idea of how far we had to go.

'Keep going, we need to keep going,' one man panted, and it was comforting to hear another human being's voice.

'You all right? Come on,' I said to the woman whose hand I had held. I still hadn't caught a look at her face and I didn't know her from Adam but she had become a 'friend in need' at that moment, united as we were through adversity, simply because of the horrors we were experiencing.

Images kept bouncing off the walls – the tunnel reminded me of a recurring dream that I had experience since about the age of 12, right up until I was around 33. What the hell was happening? What were these strange images I was seeing and why? Why now?

There was so little light that I remember straining my eyes to try to get more of an idea of where we were heading. I could make out the grainy forms of the other people who were in our little line but that was all. I clung onto the sounds of voices – they were the lifeline we all needed to hear.

'The ambulances will be waiting for us when we get out of here,' I promised my new friend. 'We'll be OK, I'm sure, we will be OK. I could feel the mice that lived in the caverns of the London Underground scampering over my feet and I could hear their high-pitched squeals. I was trying to step around them so I wouldn't tread on any – the thought of accidentally treading on one was quite horrific. I couldn't face being responsible for their death, which may sound strange but, in my heightened state of anxiety and stress, I couldn't bear the thought. I could barely swallow because of the blood in my mouth from my shattered jaw but I tried not to panic – I was afraid that, if I did, I would go on lockdown and not get out of there.

As we carried on slowly trudging through the smoky tunnel, my heart started to pound as the smells became much worse. The flashes of my recurring dream invaded my mind again. Why on earth was that?

My head started to ache now – a dull pain a bit like a bad toothache and, with it, I felt like I was going to throw up. Nothing seemed real to me. The smoke reminded me of that horrible, dense dry ice they release at the end of the night in a club while young lovers dance cheek-to-cheek and steal a last kiss before the journey home. I couldn't see my hand in front of me but I could feel the damp tiled walls and they felt strangely familiar to me. Everything about the place seemed very familiar, from the smell of urine to the swirling smoke, and the strange wafts of perfume that permeated what little air existed in the tunnel.

The flashes – they started again. This time, my mind started to race along with my heart and I began to see

pictures in my head that I didn't remember seeing before. I could see myself in someone's house and there were lots of older men around, surrounded by young boys and girls, me being one of them. I could smell the breath of one of the men as he leaned forward to kiss me on the lips and pushed me awkwardly to the floor as he unbuttoned his trousers. I was so frightened as I tried to keep my mind on where I was going but something horrible and disgusting was happening in my head.

It was a unique situation, which I couldn't make head or tail of at the time. I just remember the extreme fear of not just trying to get out of the tunnel to safety but also of trying to understand where the acute pictures in my head were coming from. The constant flashing images of me as a teenager surrounded by older men would have been disturbing at any time but, in my fragile state, when all I wanted to do was survive, I found that they were absolutely hideous.

I still don't know how long it took us to get out of that tunnel but, at 9.20am, 20 or so of us struggled out onto the platform at Russell Square. Instead of the waiting ambulances and medical help that I had expected, what greeted us was total confusion – shocked London Underground staff and commuters who didn't have a clue what was happening at that moment. The noise was unbearable – people shouting, screaming, crying, calling. I don't think anyone knew what was going on. By this time all trains on the London Underground network had been halted – no one was going to get on or off another train until further notice. I guess this was the rule until the police

and the country's intelligence networks figured out what was going on.

After we left the tunnel, I tried calling 999 but all the circuits were busy so I attempted to call 112, the unique emergency number for the whole of the European Union. At the time, only around one in five Europeans knew it existed but, due to my ties with European companies over the years, I was one of them. This number is reserved for moments when you can't get through to your own police force – such as during a natural disaster or a terrorist attack.

After that phone call, I desperately tried calling Tina but she didn't pick up. Tina, of course, knew that I would have been on that Tube line that morning and might very well have taken that very train, and I thought she would have seen the news or heard about it from her patients at the hospital. And I knew she would be panicking, not knowing if I was dead or alive. I left her a brief message, saying that I was OK, that I was alive and that I loved her very much. Next, I called my colleague from work, Peter. He was heading into the office and was just outside our work building, Lynton House.

'Peter, I'm injured and I can't get into work,' I said through tears. 'My Olympic presentation is in my office. Can you show it and go through the slides you have, please? I'll be back into work as soon as I can.' I know it sounds weird that I was so focused on my work but, in the crisis, my job was my normality and I needed that to get myself together. Besides, I had no idea of the exact extent of the terrorist attack at that point.

'What the bloody hell is going on?' he asked me and, as he said it, I heard a huge explosion in the background.

'What the fuck was that?' I screamed.

Peter was shouting in sheer panic. 'Oh my God, there's a bus that's gone up. It's been blown up! And there's a woman's hand – a finger flew through the air. Oh my God, oh my God!'

As we were speaking, 18-year-old suicide bomber Hasib Hussain had detonated his bomb while he travelled on a double-decker bus, killing 13 commuters and himself. It was the final act of terrorism on that July morning and, as a result of my phone conversation with Peter at that exact moment, I am the only victim of the bombings who was party to two explosions.

And as I sat there on the dusty station platform, dazed after the phone call to Peter, I saw dozens of frantic people trying to phone their loved ones but, for some reason, for several hours after the terrorist attack, many survivors were unable to reach people because the mobile-phone networks were all down. To say people were in agony is an understatement – all everyone wanted was to hear their loved one's comforting voices, to tell them they were still alive, to be able to say that they would be going home that night. And later we found out that there were so many people who didn't make it home for dinner that night.

As I walked out of the station covered in blood, I looked up at the sky. It was quite a miserable day with grey skies and it was faintly drizzling. The feel of that drizzle on my bloody face was such a comfort because it was a reminder that I wasn't dead – that I had somehow made it. I didn't

think about the horrific injuries – or have any idea about the mild brain damage – that I had sustained on that terrible day. All I could think was that I was alive to see another bloody awful day of British weather. And that meant everything to me – it really did.

I looked around outside the train station for a taxi or something to get me home. There were three other ladies there and we all got into the one taxi to drive us out of London.

'Listen, love,' the taxi driver said. 'I don't take credit cards or cheques – I need the cash.' So there we all were, frantically searching for cash in our purses to pay this taxi driver, who didn't have a clue what was going on either, I like to think. We pooled together the exact fare of £46.50 and he said that would take us to the end of the A10, then we would have to get out.

It was better than nothing. At that point, all we wanted to do was to get out of the city centre and the possibility of any more danger. The scenes on the roads were of chaos. It felt like everyone had gone into the city that day – there were vehicles everywhere and, as a result, there were bottleneck traffic jams wherever you looked. Thankfully, I managed to get through to Tina on the phone but literally only for a couple of seconds, to tell her that I was OK and that I was heading up the A10 towards Enfield. She sounded panic stricken and had already left the hospital to come and find me because she hadn't been able to get through to speak to me before. The sound of relief in her voice made me want to cry my heart out but I knew that, if I did, I wouldn't be able to stop.

Our taxi driver stopped the cab as soon as the money ran out – he wouldn't take us closer to the hospitals, which I was so angry about because I was covered in blood and he could see I needed help. I headed towards Enfield High Street because I felt sure that there would be someone to help me there and at least that's where Tina might look for me. As I walked down the street, it was hard to believe that I'd almost just been killed in a terrorist explosion. I staggered in a bit of a daze and people who passed me looked at me awkwardly as if I was some common drunk. No one seemed to put two and two together and recognise that I was a bomb survivor – maybe the full force of the bombings hadn't filtered through to Enfield yet.

All I knew as I looked out for Tina was that I was lucky to be alive and I wasn't going to rest until either she found me or I made it to a hospital where I would receive medical attention.

CHAPTER TWO

A GIFT BABY

Most parents believe that their child is a gift but I really was a 'gift' baby.

You see, I was born to my grandmother Sarah Stoneman and given up at seven months of age to my sister Christine and her husband Peter Rhodes.

In those days, when adoption laws were strict and costly, it was called 'gifting' your baby or handing over parental responsibility to new parents, as if the child 'was born to the adopter in lawful wedlock'.

It was 33 years before I found out the truth about my upbringing. You can imagine what finding out that most of my life had been a lie did to me.

Of course, there was the anger and the confusion that Christine Rhodes wasn't my mother but, the more I looked back over my childhood, the more it made sense to me. And the more I found out about the truth through my own

investigations, the more I realised that, even though Sarah Stoneman gave up her parental rights to me, she still loved me as her own child.

Sarah and my birth-father George had five kids before I came along – Cyril, the eldest, then Christine, Eileen, Shirley and Rex.

Her sister – whose name I don't know – had been rushed into the hospital while heavily pregnant with her daughter and, while she was in there, doctors found a tumour the size of a small beach ball that was sharing her insides with her baby.

Thankfully, both my aunt and her baby survived but, while this was going on, Sarah's stomach started growing, gradually at first. Her back ached for days on end and she became convinced that she had a tumour in her tummy just as her sister had.

It never occurred to her that she might be pregnant. She was getting on a bit to be having more children – she was in her late forties – and she already had five beautiful, healthy children. Neither she nor George wanted any more kids and that extra mouth to feed.

Sarah was so convinced that she was seriously ill that she went to see her GP with a suitcase packed and ready to take to the local hospital, Plymouth General, to have the tumour removed.

'Shall I go straight to hospital now?' she asked her doctor.

'Oh, no!' he said. 'You can have the baby at home. No need for hospitals!'

I can only imagine the scene in the doctor's surgery

when my birth-mother found out that she was five or six months pregnant.

'But I'm too old to have a baby!' she had cried, although I don't think she was much more than 48. Back then, however, women rarely had babies that late in life.

I've since also found out that for a long time Sarah had been deeply ashamed that she was pregnant. I was probably the very last viable egg she produced before she hit the menopause and bingo! She was having me! But for reasons only known to herself, she felt she had no other choice other than to try to hide the pregnancy and then to get rid of her baby as quietly as possible.

My sister Christine and her husband had been trying for at least five years to have a baby, since they got married in 1954. Christine was angry and disappointed that she couldn't produce an heir for Peter and they had started making enquiries about formal adoption.

So Sarah made them her offer – a baby to call their own, to look after forever. A child who would have their name, not the fruit of their loins but otherwise completely theirs.

They couldn't say no and they waited eagerly for my arrival for the next four months.

In the early evening of 2 August 1961, Sarah was home in Plympton, a tiny town just five miles from Plymouth, washing the dinner dishes when her waters broke all over the kitchen floor and her contractions started.

She managed to drag herself upstairs to the bedroom while my father went to fetch the midwife and, two hours later, I made my entrance into the world: a dark-haired,

extra-long, perfect baby girl. I was greeted by a jovial Sarah looking into my little face, 'Hello, my darlin'!' she said in her thickest Cornish accent. 'Hello, my liddle lover! What do we 'ave 'ere then?'

'You've a lovely baby girl!' the midwife pronounced.

Sarah didn't get overexcited. Having babies for her was like shelling peas. She had a cup of tea while the midwife delivered the afterbirth, then she was up again quickly, as if not much had happened, let alone the miracle of creating a new life.

My life.

I don't know how quickly I was handed over to Christine and Peter but my first baby photo is of me with Christine, aged about six months. We are in the back garden of her two-up two-down terrace house in Plympton, and she is holding me sideways to the camera, rather like a prize she's showing off.

Those earliest memories are the best I have of my childhood, even though they are a little vague and I think sometimes I've remembered them as better experiences that they actually were at the time, so as to protect myself.

Christine adored me at first, of that I am sure. She had the best pram for me – one of those navy-blue Silver Cross models with the enormous white wheels. Princess Margaret, who had her son Lord Linley on 3 November 1961, had one of those at the time and they were considered to be the very best prams you could buy.

I was treated like a baby doll. I was always dressed in the most fashionable, girly clothes and sometimes I would wear two or three outfits in one day. Christine loved to

keep up with the trends and Peter, who had a construction business, let her spend their money on whatever she wanted for me, the apple of her eye.

She forked out a small fortune on the first automatic pram rocker – a machine that attached to the pram handle and plugged into the wall, then gently rocked me to sleep. It was a luxury item, but nothing was ever too good for me and, besides, whatever Christine wanted, she was allowed.

Peter was out of the house most of the time. At the time he had a very successful business building houses and extensions to people's homes. He was a master builder, which meant he could turn his hand to anything at all and he was often asked by other builders to oversee jobs or give them his expert opinion. It seemed he was always running here and there in his blue Morris Minor car, catching up on jobs and errands, while leaving Christine to do the 'woman's work' of looking after kids, cooking, cleaning and making his life a lot easier.

I remember he was always making Christine something and he was a dab hand at DIY around the house. Christine was frequently asking him to make something she had seen in a magazine or on the TV. He made her beautiful kitchen cabinets, he put home-made shelves on the walls where she showed-off her ornaments, and he even made the frames for our photographs.

One year he made a big Christmas tree out of wood and he hung it from the ceiling in our lounge by a nail. Another time he made Christine a kidney-shaped dressing table and a chair. They were all the rage with the big movie stars and

Peter even attached a pretty little frill around it, just like in the pictures that Christine had seen.

She loved that dressing table like it was the Crown Jewels. She set her perfume bottles and jewellery on the table and she would sit for hours brushing her hair in the mirror and doing her make-up. I swear she had ideas of one day being famous and having all the riches that went with it. She was lucky that Peter made such a good living allowing her to spend money as she did.

Peter was a good father to me – well, at least for the first four years of my life. When he came home from work in the evenings, we would play my favourite game, called 'Lumpy'. I would sit on his knee and, holding the dog's lead, I would ride Peter like he was a horse.

I would scream, 'Lumpy, lumpy, lumpy!' as Peter would bounce me up and down, higher and higher, until I would almost fall off. I loved that game and I loved being with the man who I thought for all that time was my father. The Lumpy game was our fun time and he never ever told me we couldn't play, no matter how tired he was after a long day's work.

He would make me little gifts too. One of them was a tall wooden stool that I would climb up on to get to the kitchen work surface. From there, I could reach the food cupboards and the sink if I needed to wash my hands. I know he'd given it to me to make their lives easier – I was much more mobile and able to help myself with the stool – but I loved that stool because it was all mine. He brought it for me and I didn't have to share it with anybody.

Everything I loved about my childhood ended abruptly when I was four years old and, by some kind of a miracle, Christine had her daughter Tracy. I say a miracle because both Christine and Peter had been told in no uncertain terms by the doctor that they couldn't have their own kids. I think that they had given up and, as they were happy with me, they stopped trying for a baby of their own. You read about this natural phenomenon all the time these days – couples stop IVF and stop beating themselves up every month trying to conceive, then the woman gets pregnant naturally, once all the stress is gone.

Unfortunately for us all, little Tracy was the child from hell and, after having such an easy time with me as a baby, Christine and Peter got the shock of their lives when their blonde-haired, blue-eyed little girl was born.

From the moment she arrived, she didn't sleep. Not ever. Not even for an hour here and there. She cried and complained the whole time and nothing settled her. Christine would try cuddling her when she got upset, she'd put her in the bath with nice soothing hot water, she would dance around the lounge with her while singing to her, desperately trying to get her to calm down and sleep.

I remember once – I think Tracy was about five months old – Christine called the doctor. Tracy was teething and she never stopped screaming. I guess Christine and Peter were at the end of their tether with it. The doctor came round and he gave both Christine and Tracy medication to help them both to sleep.

'Take these and try to get some rest. You look terrible,' the doctor told Christine. And she did; she looked like

death warmed up. The enormous dark rings she had around her eyes made her look like a panda, her skin was sallow at times and, at other times, as white as a sheet, and her hair looked like it hadn't been brushed in months.

Christine had always taken pride in her appearance but, when Tracy was born, the make-up quickly disappeared, as did the trendy clothes. She rarely took a bath, instead having quick 'strip washes' in the kitchen sink, which she hated. 'All I want is a bath,' she said once, through tears. 'Just a thirty-minute bath to myself, where I can switch off and forget about everything. It's not a lot to ask.' She more often than not dressed in big baggy clothes that did nothing to show off her slim, enviable figure. After Tracy arrived, she turned into a shadow of her former self in every way possible. I think that's what sleep deprivation will do to you.

As soon as Tracy came along, I was pushed out of my bedroom to make room for her. My room was transformed into a beautiful pink palace fit for a princess, complete with every toy imaginable. Peter renovated the loft and set me up in there. It was lonely up there and I didn't like it because Peter hadn't even painted it, but at least at night I could barely hear Tracy's screams, so I managed to get a lot more sleep than her parents, at least. It was ironic though because, for the first two or three years of her life, Tracy was so unsettled that she never moved out of their bedroom into her own.

The trouble was, with every day that she didn't get her sleep, Christine took out her anger and frustrations on me, probably because I was such an easy target. She would

have me help her fill our top-loader washing machine with clothes and then two hours later have me drag them out and into the dryer. Sometimes I had to help her fold the clothes, other times I was told to watch my sister while she tried to make the dinner. Unfortunately, I was no good as a babysitter, probably because I was no more than a toddler myself and I could do little to calm down the screaming child.

If I didn't do as I was told, or if I didn't do it quickly enough, I would be beaten with the wooden spoon. Christine had a collection of wooden spoons she kept in her kitchen drawer and, gosh, those things could hurt when she used them on me during one of her temper tantrums.

'Do you want the wooden spoon?' she would say menacingly. If I didn't reply quickly enough, she would whack me with it anyway and she didn't care where she got me. I regularly got hit across my face, on the back of my legs, across my chest or head, around my ears or on my back. She didn't care that someone might see me with big welt marks on my skin. I think she couldn't cope with Tracy, so I was her beating post – it was as simple as that. Peter must have seen my thrashings but he never told her to stop.

Looking back, I am sure that Tracy would have been diagnosed with something like ADHD or autism or some other form of hyperactivity but, back then, there were no names you could put to whatever it was that Tracy was suffering from. Christine and Peter were in the dark and there was very little help that they could get to help them

cope with such a demanding child. Tracy grew into a toddler who never gave anybody two minutes' peace, who was constantly on the go and who needed stimulating all the time.

I credit my real mum, Sarah, with saving this small part of my childhood. She lived just 20 minutes from us and, as soon as Tracy was born and she started creating problems, Sarah was round our house almost every day to help out. It was quite obvious from the look of Christine and the way her once-tidy house had collapsed into a dishevelled pile of dirty nappies, unclean floors and half-cooked food that she needed some serious help. It was during this time that Nana Sarah and I became incredibly close and she became very protective of me. Whenever she could, she lavished me with the attention I was so missing from my parents.

Of course, I couldn't see this at the time. All I knew was that, when Nana Sarah came round to our house, my day just got a whole lot better. Often her way of helping Christine out was to take me out of the way and we would go out for the afternoon, just the two of us. I was allowed to be a carefree kid again, to laugh and not to be afraid that, if I did something the least bit wrong, I would get beaten with a wooden spoon.

Sarah took me for walks in the local forest, where she would point out all the beautiful trees and flowers. We would go for a trip to the beach and laugh while eating giant cones with a chocolate flake and raspberry sauce piled onto the ice-cream – they were called 99s, I seem to remember. I loved her to take me berry or mushroom

picking with our little baskets, being extra careful not to get pricked or stung. Often we would go for picnics in the sunshine, or she would take me to the village chapel, where we would sit holding hands, chatting to each other and talking to God.

We had our own secret language. Sarah was actually rather well educated and she was fluent in speaking the native Cornish language, which is very difficult to learn. She taught me Cornish so well that, by the time I was five, I was fluent in Cornish and English. When we were together – particularly in the house – we would talk in Cornish, much to the annoyance of Christine, who hated that we shared this secret way of chatting.

'Will you two please speak proper English!' Christine would demand as we giggled to each other. 'It's really bloody annoying, Mother! Nobody else speaks Cornish around here and I don't want Beverli speaking it!'

Sarah and I would give each other a knowing look and a smile, then we would talk English for a bit before slipping back into Cornish. I loved it that we shared such a simple bond. Tracy took up so much of Christine's attention that there was never any time for me. The only person who gave me the time I deserved was Sarah and I will be forever grateful to her because she made all the difference to my young life.

Of course, now I know why we had that special bond. They say that the love a mother feels for her child never goes away, no matter what happens in their lives. Christine could beat me and hurt me and treat me like the skivvy because that mother-daughter bond was never

there – and she couldn't fake it, especially not when her own biological daughter came along. I think that, after Tracy arrived, I rarely ever got a kiss goodnight or a bedtime story from Christine or Peter. I was never again showed an ounce of love from the woman I believed was my mother.

Sarah died never knowing that I knew that she was my mother – that all came out when Christine was sick years later with breast cancer. I was 34 years old when she was diagnosed with a condition nicknamed the 'galloping cancer' by doctors, because it was so fast spreading. It had started in her breast and, within just a few months, had spread to her organs, her bones and then her brain. I went back to live with her, to nurse her in her final few weeks, as I felt a good daughter should look after her mother, even if she hadn't really been much of a mother to me.

One day, she dropped it in conversation that Tracy was going to be coming home to help as well and that she had to have the bedroom where I had been sleeping during my stay. I couldn't believe it! I had been there for weeks looking after Christine while Tracy had got on with her life. Christine wasn't an easy patient either, always so full of orders and requests that I had to put my own job on hold to look after her full time.

I admit I went mad when I heard that I had to give up my bed for Tracy. 'Do you know what, Mum?' I said to Christine. 'Why don't you just let Tracy look after you now because I'm going. I am sick of all this favouritism – I've lived with it all my life and now I'm done with it all. I'm leaving

you!' Christine was visibly upset at this confrontation and she still denied the truth up until the day she died.

'You don't have to go,' she said. 'Don't be stupid, Beverli.' I was so angry with her right then. 'Why don't you just admit that you would rather have Tracy with you?' I asked. 'Go on, admit it!'

She refused to admit anything. Instead, she gave me a paper that she had signed. 'Before you go, I need you to take this to the bank and withdraw all my money,' she said as she handed me a withdrawal slip for the sum of £40,000 – her savings. 'Why on earth do you want me to get this money out?' I asked. 'Well, Tracy needs the money – she needs to get a house and a car. This will help her.' As I was listening to all this, it was like adding insult to injury. Christine had never offered me money – not that I wanted it or needed it – but I was damned if Tracy was going to get it all. We were sisters and that meant we shared everything.

'What has she been telling you for you to think that she's so hard done by?' I asked, my temper rising again.

'Well, she is my daughter, you know,' Christine said.

'I know that but what about me, Mum?' I asked. 'What do I get in your will?'

Christine looked me in the eye and said, quite coldly, 'You aren't my daughter.'

That stopped me dead in my tracks.

'I don't understand,' I said, confused. 'Of course I'm your daughter.' I thought that maybe she was delirious because of all the medications she was on, but she was lucid.

'Tracy is my only child,' said Christine. 'You've never been my real daughter.'

I could see in her face that she was telling me the truth, that she wasn't trying to hurt me by lying, and, after she died, she left a note saying the exact same thing, along with Sarah's name written down as my real mother. For the first time in my life everything started to make sense. The fact that Christine never bothered with me after Tracy was born and that I was always second best to her was because I wasn't really a part of that little family at all. At best, I was Christine's much younger sister, and it didn't seem like that fact had ever meant anything to her either. It took me years to come to terms with the fact that most of my life had been a sham – an enormous lie – and I questioned who I really was.

Now, after a lot of therapy and counselling, I am at peace with what happened, although I shall never forgive Christine for treating me with such little feeling or care. I may not have been her daughter but I was still a little girl who needed to be loved, looked after and kept safe. Christine did none of those things for me and I often wish that Sarah had never given me away. It would have been far better to have been brought up by a much older woman who loved me, than by a young wife who didn't.

To this day, I wish with all my heart I'd had the opportunity to tell Sarah that I knew who she was while she was alive. Even though I never did, I will always refer to and think of her as my mother because, as a very young child, when I needed to feel loved the most,

she was the one who showed me that attention and affection that I yearned for in my life. I will always love her for that.

CHAPTER THREE

IN THE
BEGINNING

After Tracy arrived in the world, I felt that I had lost the woman who I considered to be my mother. Peter was the one who took care of me the most, whenever he was at home.

Tracy was born in September 1964, when I was just three years old. On the day that she was born, Christine's mother, Sarah, looked at the leaves in her teacup and she saw that they were arranged in a most unusual way.

'There's a bleeding here in the tea leaves at the bottom of the cup!' she exclaimed. She looked at Christine and then at me. 'That doesn't do!' she exclaimed. 'That's not a good sign! I wonder why.'

I think that she knew in her heart of hearts that something wasn't going to be right with this baby girl. Sarah had always had an inner knowledge of all things psychic

and mystical and she swore blind that the tea leaves were always right.

I don't remember where Tracy was born – I don't even remember Christine being pregnant. I just remember that she appeared one day and that life as I knew it changed forever. She wasn't a particularly pretty baby. She was like a white bowling ball, with no hair and very pale eyebrows; so pale you could barely see them. That day she was quiet, as I stared hard at her, not knowing whether to touch her or to recoil in horror!

Then, when I turned four, I became aware that Peter was taking more notice of me than before. It started that winter after Tracy arrived.

He would insist on bathing me. He would push the assumption that I was still too young to bathe myself and that looking after me when she had Tracy was a great inconvenience for Christine. So Christine was always quite happy to leave me for Peter to sort out. Often I would hear Christine say to close friends and family, 'That man is a diamond, a real jewel of a man!' as if she completely adored him and was so thankful for his presence. She would share that Peter would peel the spuds and get the vegetables ready for Sunday dinner as the meat roasted – apparently, he would even wash up all the pots and the heavy roasting tin.

Everyone would be in awe of Christine. 'What a lucky girl you are to have found such a fine man,' people would say time and again. Of course, in those days, women were chained to the kitchen and the kids while the men went out to work – it was just the way of the world. Peter being such

a help around the house was very different and I am sure Christine's female friends and her family would have loved a Peter for themselves. If only they knew, though, the hidden reasons behind him being so accommodating.

Night after night, I'd sit in the pale-pink bath tub, playing happily, and he would sit on the side, chatting to me, quite normally really.

'Have you washed your hair?' he'd ask, knowing full well I didn't know how to do that yet, so he would grab the shampoo bottle and wash my shoulder length hair, then rinse it afterwards. Then he would take the sponge or the face cloth, covered in bubbles, and wash me all over my body. He was quite gentle on my back, my neck and my legs but, when it came to my private areas and my bottom, he was quick and I was done in no time.

It was as if nothing was private between me and Peter.

I could be sitting on the toilet and he would walk straight in and start shaving. Or he would look at me, sitting there, knickers around my ankles, swinging my legs and leaning over the edge of the loo. He would stare for a few seconds before sticking his head in the sink to quickly wash his hair.

Of course, back then we had one tiny, poky bathroom with a bath, sink and a toilet in there so, if anyone was desperate for the loo and you were the person on it, you had to hurry up!

I wasn't allowed to lock the door for obvious reasons, for instance I might get trapped in the room if the lock stuck, so it was easy for Peter just to waltz in whenever he wanted to.

Although it was a bit embarrassing at first, I didn't mind and it became so commonplace that I didn't ever think it was strange. It never occurred to me that my own father shouldn't really be in the bathroom while I was on the toilet.

But that was just how it was and even bedtimes were also just Peter and me alone.

'Chris, I'll put Beverli to bed,' he'd say, particularly if she was having a hard time with Tracy. 'Don't you worry about her – all you need to do is to think about Tracy.'

By this time, Christine had shrunk from an ample, busty ten to eleven stone, fairly strong, well-endowed woman to a six-stone shadow of her former self.

With all the sleepless nights and the anxiety that Tracy brought with her, I guess Christine's own body couldn't cope with the stress and the pounds had fallen off her.

She rarely had time to eat, sleep or rest and I am sure that, even though she adored her Tracy, she secretly wished that she had been blessed with a more manageable, happy baby.

She really was a nervous wreck and Peter took full advantage of her state of mind. Looking back, Tracy was the best thing that could have happened for Peter because he was free to be alone around me much, much more than if I'd been an only child and I'd had a mother who cared.

At bedtime, he would sometimes read me a story and always undress me, slipping my nightie over my body and tucking me into bed. Often he would make me wear my cosy, warm flannelette dressing gown and, for a short time, the warmth he showed me made me feel wanted and loved and that I belonged to the family as much as Tracy did.

In a way, I loved him being there because, even though I was just four, I had noticed that Christine wasn't around as much and that the world revolved around my screaming, annoying little sister. I liked the attention from Peter, who, despite being so busy with work, always made time for me.

At the time, Peter did a lot of work for a company called Marley Tiles, in Plymouth, as well as numerous side jobs to bring in extra money, and he held different positions within the Freemasons' Society in our little town, including Treasurer.

Everybody liked Peter and regarded him highly. He was a dark-haired man with a full head of curly black hair, bright, shining eyes that were almost grey sometimes and, at other time, light blue, depending on the light. He was dashingly handsome in an old-school film-star kind of way, with straight, white teeth and a strong jawline. He had a very coy way of speaking, in a low, soft voice, with a syrup-sweet sexiness that seemed win over everyone he talked to, male or female. He was very confident, sometimes to the point of arrogance, and extremely outgoing. He would drop whatever he was doing at the time if one of his Brothers in his Freemasons lodge called him to organise something like a Ladies' Evening for the wives or a benefit for their members, or even just to visit a Mason in hospital and provide support for his family. He would even sort out funerals and aftercare for the widows of the surviving families if something happened such as the death of a child. So you can see that he was regarded as a genuinely caring man who would help anybody.

As a result, he had a lot of friends. Often on a Saturday

lunchtime, people would turn up at our house and help Peter clean the car or work on the garden while they drank bottles of beer and had a laugh. He treated them like they were part of our family, his Freemason brothers-in-arms.

On these occasions Christine would be inside looking after Tracy and Peter would be getting his down time with his friends, which I am sure was perfect for him. I would either be inside playing with my Barbie dolls or the farmyard animals I had begun to collect. The little animals were made of pewter and, when Peter took me into Plymouth with him shopping, he would buy me a new foal or a chicken or a horse, or whatever caught my eye because he knew how much I loved playing with them and, eventually, they became a good tool to get me to do things for him.

Sometimes I would play in the front garden with my dollies, watching what was going on with Peter and his friends. I was familiar with everyone who came to our house and I looked on them as my uncles. I had a lot of uncles back then.

One day – it must have been late spring because I was in a little pale-pink dress, which looked a bit like the special dress that Cinderella wore to the ball in the Disney film – I remember waking up to a light drizzle of rain, which later cleared up to make way for brilliant sunshine and a rather hot day. I was sitting on the front lawn, playing with my dollies when Peter called me over.

He was washing the car with three of his friends. There were soap suds everywhere and the hose pipe was turned on. One of the men was buffing the tyres of Peter's navy-

blue Morris Minor with boot polish, taking extra care to miss the tyre's white areas – that car was Peter's pride and joy and everyone knew it.

'You can play in the water if you like,' said the man and I started to splash around in the bubbles made by the washing-up liquid they were using to wash the car. I was laughing loudly and having so much fun.

'Don't get your shoes wet,' Peter shouted to me. 'Your mother won't like that – you'll get me into trouble!'

I heard him clearly – he had a specific warning tone in his voice – and I was careful but I didn't stop splashing around. I was having way too much of a good time. Like all kids of that age, I loved messing around in water, especially where there were bubbles.

Then he took me to one side. 'Beverli, we need a cloth to wash and polish the car,' he said. 'I'm not going through the house to the kitchen – your mum will kill me if I leave wet and dirty footprints through the house. Take your knickers off and I'll use them.'

So I pulled my dress up, took off my knickers and handed them to Peter, no questions asked.

The thought of him going into the house and risking waking up Tracy or getting on Christine's nerves was horrible. I had often seen them have rows over the stupidest of things, like leaving the door open, not closing the fridge properly, not doing the dishes well – silly things that Christine wouldn't have worried or got angry about if she wasn't so sleep deprived and depressed. I didn't want Peter to go through the house and risk yet another row that would, potentially, spoil our afternoon because,

when Christine was in a bad mood, it was not only Peter that got the wrath of her temper; it was usually me too.

After I'd handed over my knickers, Peter gave them to one of his friends and he slipped them into his pocket. I thought he must be taking them home to use on his own car later. To me, it was all so innocent.

Later, Peter took me into my bedroom. He went straight to my knicker drawer and chose a pair near the bottom of the pile. Calmly and with intent, he lifted my hem, grabbed each leg and pushed them into each leg of my knickers. Then, ever so fast, he yanked them up around my waist and fluffed the bottom to make sure all was straight and its place, just how it should be. Peter then let me go and he dashed downstairs and out of the house to be back with his guests, as if nothing out of the ordinary had happened. And I was back to normal with a clean pair of knickers on, so all was well with the world.

'If you don't tell your mother about this, next time I clean the car you can put your swimsuit on and play in the spray if you like,' he had said before dashing downstairs.

That was enough to keep my silence for ever and I never told Christine. It was our little secret and the handing over of my knickers started to become a regular event when his friends came to our house.

Every time he would ask, 'Can Uncle so-and-so have your knickers to wash his car because they clean so well?' And I would willingly hand them over right there and then, knowing that, if I did, I would get a friendly smile from whoever the 'uncle' was and Peter would be nice to me for the rest of the day.

Every man who I met through Peter was called 'Uncle' and there seemed to be always one uncle who needed a pair of my knickers to clean his car.

Sometimes Peter would take my dirty knickers out of my bedroom after I'd gone to bed or he'd steal them out of the washing basket. Other times, if I'd had a strip wash in the sink the night before rather than having a proper bath, and I'd worn the same knickers for two days, he would take them too, regardless of how dirty they were.

Many years later, I found out that he was making a small fortune by selling my underwear to his friends and they weren't using them to polish their cars either. I heard that, for the two-day-old knickers, he could get £20 a time.

Christine never knew that my underwear was missing because Peter covered his tracks well. He'd take me into Woolworths in Plymouth and buy me a whole load of new panties regularly, so that my old supply was always replenished. He would wash and bleach them, then place them neatly in my drawer as if Christine had done it.

Christine was a complete cleanliness fanatic, especially after Tracy was born. Every item of underwear was bleached, along with work surfaces in the kitchen, the bathrooms, the floors – even the walls were regularly scrubbed when she made the time. She would tie old torn-up towels dipped in bleach onto the toilet chain and handle, then leave them overnight to clean. She would scrub the sinks with a mixture of baby oil and cotton wool to get rid of the scratches – it worked a treat too.

So my knickers never looked old, always smelled of bleach and Christine never knew any different. She had no

idea that her lovely new bookcase or curtains had probably been paid for by my dirty underwear.

At around the same time, Peter started taking me to people's houses for film afternoons with other kids. It was often a different house but always in the same area and we would go usually around lunchtime to meet his friends.

The windows always shut off any view of inside the room from the outside world, using temporary blackout blinds and a white sheet that was hung from the pelmets, just to make completely sure no one could see in.

I don't know if Peter organised these parties but he always knew everyone who was there. Sometimes there were as many as 10 or 12 men who arrived at different times, often with their children in tow.

For us children, it was great fun and something to really look forward to. We were of all ages too – I think the youngest child was a little girl who was only about 18 months old – she was toddling all over the place and I loved watching her.

There was always this one little boy who came – he must have been about two-and-a-half. He would get a little erection – I don't know whether someone showed him how to stimulate himself, but he would run around the room screaming with laughter, his little penis waggling up and down as he did so.

Sometimes he'd use his hand to stimulate himself more. And of course, although small, he still had very much a penis, just like a miniature version of those attached to the men, who were also feeling themselves as they watched the young boy's every move. They just sat there, all of them, hands

down trousers all the time, with their steely eyes boring into him as they watched the little lad's innocent game as he laughed with delight at his spectators. All the men thought this was hilarious too, as if it was the most normal thing in the world to be doing. I just remember thinking it looked weird and wondering why it was so funny – why was he running around without his nappy on for all of them to see his private parts? I just didn't understand what was going on.

The film afternoons always played out the same each time we went. First of all, we were allowed to watch cartoons – usually *Bugs Bunny* or *Tom and Jerry*, and always *Looney Toons* – beamed onto a wall in the living room by a big projector. The cartoons were on the small reels, which were played first as a prelude to the larger reels that provided the main show.

We would be given unlimited amounts of sweet tea, Victoria sponge cakes or other pastries and as many sweets as we could eat while we watched our cartoons in the blackened room.

The adults would be seated on the settees and chairs and us kids would sit on knees or on the arms of the furniture, but rarely on the floor. It seemed that the men didn't mind at all if we sat really close to them.

After the cartoons, it was like musical chairs. Often we would be called to sit on 'Uncle Somebody's' knee while they put their films on, and no one ever said no. To be honest, after eating such a lot of treats, it wasn't uncommon for us to become drowsy or fall asleep on laps. I still do wonder if anything was added to our sweet tea to help us to relax.

The adult films were porn – often hardcore porn.

I remember watching a film once where the man was holding down a woman and raping her. 'Why is she screaming, Daddy?' I asked Peter. 'Is he hurting her?' I didn't understand and neither did most of the other kids.

'No, she's fine,' Peter said, without even trying to elaborate.

Often during the porn films, the grown-ups would take a child to the toilet and be gone for ages. Or they would take a tired child into a bedroom on the pretence of putting them down for a nap, and then they would come back a few minutes later to finish watching the film.

I was always a favourite with the older men of the group, maybe because I was really quite petite and quiet – they seemed to love that about me.

'Come and give Uncle Eddie a hug and a kiss,' Peter would say and I'd have to sit on their knee while they kissed and hugged me. It didn't matter to me that I did that a lot – the men were perfectly pleasant and I guess you could say that they brought my love and affection with sweets, dollies and toys.

If the 'uncle' was someone I had never met before, or I didn't like him, he would do everything to gain my trust and make me take to him. Often, they would play the Lumpy game with me, when I would ride their legs like horses. I loved that game so much and I thought, if they liked to play it, they must be OK people. It was all part of me and the other kids being groomed by Peter and his cronies.

A favourite kind of film for the adults was real-life shows, where people have been filmed in bathing costumes

splashing around in their paddling pool, or running around half naked in the summer sun. These kinds of films seemed to really get their attention and it never ceased to amaze me how often they would nip to the loo during the viewing. I always thought they'd just drunk too much sweet tea or beer.

Sometimes we would go to someone's house for a dressing-up afternoon and I particularly loved those outings with Peter. At home I didn't have many friends and at these get-togethers I was surrounded by people my own age, so I loved the company.

We would get dressed up in whatever our parents or 'uncles' told us to. That could have been anything from a princess or prince costume to a doctor or nurse outfit. I was a pretty little nurse a lot of the time, with a black cape.

The cine camera would always come out and, as we were being filmed, we were given orders by the grown-ups in the room: 'Give the prince a kiss,' the princess would be told. 'Give him a big hug!'

As I was always a nurse, I was told to examine the 'patient' to see what was wrong with him. Someone would use lipstick to draw a heart on the naked patient's chest and I would be given my instructions by the director.

'Listen to his heart,' he would say. 'I think he needs an injection to make him feel better.'

I would be given a syringe with water in it and told to give him an injection in his bottom, which would be covered in red lipstick dots.

I remember once I was given a magnifying glass. 'Check his willy,' I was told. 'Nurse, can you find out what is

wrong with him?' And I would have to carefully look at his private parts through the glass, all the while being filmed. After the examination, I had to give him Smarties as tablets and then the boy recovered from his fake illness and everything was good again.

The filming of these scenes would be seen by a select few and, when the group came to watch them, there was always a great deal of excitement and anticipation. Some of the guys would sit with a big blanket over their laps, presumably so that they could masturbate in private – although it wasn't really private because there were always children everywhere.

I always knew when the film afternoon had been a success because Peter was in a good mood.

'Let's stop off for some fish-and-chips,' he'd say. 'Give your mum a nice break from making us tea.'

I loved calling for fish-and-chips from the 'chippy'. Somehow, they tasted all the more delicious smothered in salt and vinegar and wrapped in newspaper from the local fish-and-chip shop.

Christine would be thrilled when we got home, especially since she didn't have to cook that evening. We never ate out, so the chippy was such a big treat and she loved all kinds of fish, especially battered cod, plaice and scampi tails.

I loved the really crispy chips, so Peter would pick those out for me and put them in a big white bap with extra salt and vinegar and tomato sauce. Talk about the best chip buttie in the world! The food always felt like some kind of a reward, even though I didn't really know what for. I

just knew that it had been a really good day, Peter was happy and even Christine was somewhat happy, which meant for a nice evening watching the TV and a bedtime story from Peter.

Often on these nights, Peter would sneak my urine from the potty under my bed. He had installed it there on the pretence of me needing it in the night, although I was more than capable of running to the loo if I needed to. I was never afraid of the dark at that time – being afraid of the dark came later.

He collected my urine in little baby-food jars and sometimes glass marmalade jars. There was a section in his shed where he kept empty glass jars on a thick plank of wood. I had never really known what they were for until, one day, I saw one of them in his toolbox and it was filled with an amber-coloured liquid – my wee.

'What's that?' I asked him innocently. I don't think he really knew what to say but he told me the truth.

'It's wee,' he said. 'Sometimes I use it from the toilet and keep it to clean my old screws and nails. It's very good for that.'

It seemed like a plausible explanation to me. I was still only four, going on five, and whatever Peter said I accepted, simply because he was the person I thought of as my father and I trusted him implicitly. I thought it was a little bit weird but that was all.

Later that night, I was looking towards my mirror and there was a black 'thing' sliding down the side of it, which made me very afraid. When I tried to get across to switch on my bedroom lamp for a clearer view, it vanished into

the wall, like it knew I was coming; as if whatever it was didn't want me to see it.

I screamed and, as Peter and Christine were still awake, they dashed into my room to ask me what on earth was wrong. I told them about the thing at the side of the mirror and they dismissed what I had said as a dream. Peter even suggested that I had seen something in one of the cartoons that had given me nightmares.

'Please stay in my room,' I begged them both. 'Then you can switch off the lights and wait with me for when it comes back.' I thought that, if they could see it for themselves, they could work out what it was and assess how much danger it might pose. They did stay for a few minutes, their dark eyes straining to look at the mirror.

'For Christ's sake, Bev, this isn't funny,' Christine barked at me. I looked at the mirror, desperate for whatever it was to show itself again to prove that I wasn't lying. We sat in stony silence until I couldn't bear it any more. 'It was there, it was there, it really was!' I cried, my protest cutting through the darkness and the silence. 'Yeah, like pigs will fly in here!' Peter snapped back.

Suddenly, there was a scratching noise behind the mirror. Little paws with claws appeared around the side of it, followed by two little see-through pink ears and a long nose. It was a very small mouse that had made its home in my bedroom. I wasn't going crazy and I definitely wasn't lying. I went back to bed with the promise that they would put traps down in the morning and, as the issue of the mouse was far more pressing than why Peter was stashing my urine away, I never gave it another thought. It became

normal, like so many other aspects of my life that were, in truth, anything but.

Some nights, when Peter wanted to collect a 'sample', he would have me drink a lot so I would produce more. He would also feed me sweets – especially boiled, sugary sweets and mint humbugs – cakes and biscuits to make my urine sweeter. Some nights I could smell the sugar in my urine and, from what I know now, the sweeter the better for his clients.

I still don't know exactly what they were doing with my urine – whether it was for taking 'Golden Showers' with, or for sniffing, or even drinking – but I do know that Peter made a lot of money from selling it, otherwise he wouldn't have gone to the trouble. He never did anything that wasn't going to pay him back in some way or another and so, with the sales of my knickers and my urine, he was making quite a profit aside from his day jobs.

One of his friends who was a regular buyer of my urine was a middle-aged chap who owned a little farm holding not far from us. He was actually a very talented leather smith and he made the most exquisite handbags, purses and key rings. This man also owned horses and, in a roundabout way, I have him and his love of my urine to thank for introducing me to the world of these special animals.

Peter would take me with him when he dropped off a jar at the farm and I loved visiting the place. While the men did business and had a chat in the barn, I would be allowed to stand at the gate to the field where the horses grazed. He had two enormous Clydesdales that he used to pull a cart

with the beer kegs on, and they completely fascinated me from the moment I clapped eyes on them.

They were both big, heavy horses with enormous, majestic heads and big feathers on their legs. At home, my favourite toy was my farm and on this I had lots of plastic horses I would play with. That farm was the biggest escape for me from Christine's tempers, from Tracy's constant cries and, eventually, from Peter's weird film days, which I grew to loathe as I grew older.

I remember I would sit alone in my bedroom and bring out the farm. I'd have pigs, sheep and cows in one part of the area but in the section near the barn I had my horses. I'd sit for ages pretending that I was riding the horses over big jumps. I'd give a running commentary as I sat the spectators – or bendy people, as they were known – at the side of the grass, so that they could watch the horse shows I organised. It was pure escapism where I was free to be a child, to be who I wanted to be – and even in my wildest dreams, that was always to be a horse rider.

I had toy Clydesdales in my little set, so to meet these beautiful animals for real was such a thrill for me. I was never afraid to touch them. I only had to call and they would come sauntering over to say hello or, if they were in their stalls in the barn, Peter's friend would get one of them out for me so I could stroke its huge gentle face. Both horses would lower their heads to my level, as if they were coming specifically to me and I loved the feeling that they liked me to stroke them. They were both so quiet and calm, so reassuring that, when I was with them, my life was almost good.

At the same farm was Abigail, a 15-hands-high cob who was a beautiful red-roan colour. She was the first horse I ever sat on when I was about five years old and, from the moment I sat on that mare's back, I was totally hooked. I rode her bareback as Peter watched and his friend led us around the stable yard. The feeling of warmth from her body to mine was the best feeling I had ever had – she felt completely safe as her fluffy tummy moved from side to side and she walked slowly as if she knew she had a precious package on her back. I loved the sound of her breathing beneath me – never rushed, just comforting. She was such an honest mare, very sweet and loving – I never wanted to get off.

If I knew that Peter was visiting the 'leather guy', I would beg him to take me so that I could see the Clydesdales and Abigail. Peter more often than not took me with him and, while he talked with his friend, I would feed Abigail grass and sugar cubes beneath the fence. She would always come to me when I called her, which thrilled me no end. I was in my own little world, filled with the most glorious of horses and I longed Abigail to be my own.

Peter saw how much I loved the horses and so he persuaded Christine to let me have riding lessons. I think it was still part of what I call the 'grooming' process that started with his friends giving me sweets and toys in exchange for a nice big hug and a kiss, or a pair of my dirty knickers or a jar of sweet pee. By giving me such a pleasure in my life, he knew that it was the perfect way to keep me where he wanted me – under his rule – and riding became like a sweetener for me. I think he thought that, the more

he gave me nice things, the more compliant I would be and the more I would love and trust him.

He was right, of course. I loved Peter for bringing all these things into my life. Like any little girl who loves horses, riding lessons were the best thing to ever happen to me. I don't think Christine really cared to be honest, apart from the fact that most Saturday mornings I was with Peter at a barn and horse yard 20 odd miles away, and we wouldn't be back until lunchtime. For me, it was the highlight of my week and I counted down the days to those weekends when I could spend my hour with the horses. I felt that I could endure anything as long as the weekend arrived, the weather was fine, and I could have my time with the horses.

The barn was very kid-friendly, so I made some new friendships there, which was good for me because I didn't really have any regular companions, only the ones who attended the film afternoons. I learned to ride with two horses. The first was Jiggs, a weedy, slightly built chestnut gelding with a black mane and tail. Jiggs was all of about 14hh (hands high) with a weird gait, which meant he didn't trot like the other horses. His breeding – he was part Appaloosa – gave him a trot called an 'Indian Shuffle', which was most sought after in his breed. I liked it though because it meant that I could sit beautifully to his trot and he was so sweet that he would do more or less anything I asked him to do.

The other pony I was paired with was a little one called Woodstock, another gelding, with a very dark bay coat. It was absolutely striking to look at and he was another

funny character. He loved to pull your hair if it was done in a ponytail and, as my hair was collar length, I would tuck it into the back of my jacket whenever I picked his hooves out so he wouldn't pull it. It was just a little trick – he wasn't being mean or anything – and I loved him for it. In fact, it wouldn't have mattered who I had ridden, because I know I would have taken to them all.

Woodstock and I got on so well that we did my first show together at the barn. The owner was always organising little mini-schooling shows where us kids could practise our skills. It was a cheap way of learning how to compete and also of increasing one's confidence in the saddle. Normally, Christine wouldn't go to watch me because she found the whole experience boring and tedious but she did go to watch me in my first show, along with Peter and Tracy in her pushchair.

I remember sitting there at our house before the show in my second-hand breeches and crisp white show shirt. I watched my reflection, not only in the mirror, but also in overly clean windows and across the screen of our switched-off, rented, black-and-white television. I was trying to catch a glimpse of what I looked like before I put my green jacket on.

I recalled the vision of myself, as clear as I could in my mind, while I was mounted and ready to go into the ring. I was excited and thrilled at the same time but I knew that we would do really well in our class. We had been practising our walk, trot, canter for the previous few lessons and I was more than ready to go into the little ring in front of everybody and show off what I had

learned and my almost perfect seat. It was important to me to do well, especially as Christine was going to be there. All I wanted to do was to show her that I was good at something, perhaps to get some of the attention from Tracy and some form of acknowledgment just for me, even if it was just for an afternoon.

Woodstock and I couldn't have done any better and we went home that afternoon with our first blue ribbon – that's a first in our class of about 10 young riders. I was beyond excited when I received my rosette and even Christine seemed happy for me. Peter was especially pleased though.

'We are so proud of you!' he beamed as he hugged me. 'You and that pony are champions!'

That was one of the best days of my life up until then. The pride I felt in myself and my pony, and the hearing of such pride and joy in Peter's voice, meant the world to me, it really did, because I knew that, if I was making him happy, it was good for me too. And I also wanted more. I wanted my own pony. I wanted to live on a farm and surround myself with horses. Already, horses were becoming a big comfort in my world and I couldn't stop thinking about them, or looking forward to my lessons. I would wake up thinking about horses and go to sleep dreaming about them.

And anything that Peter asked me to do, I would willingly do in exchange for the time I spent with the horses, and he knew that. Horses had become the perfect leverage for Peter to use to 'persuade' me to do things that no child should ever have to do. He also used horses as a reward for being a 'good' girl. Although, on a spiritual

level, my life had got better because of my time with the horses, on a whole new other level, it was about to get a lot worse with Peter.

IN THE BEGINNING

level, my life had got better beyond even my dreams with the horses, on a whole new virtual level, it will about to get a whole lot more complex.

CHAPTER FOUR

IN THE NAME
OF SHAME

One of Peter's favourite 'compliments' to me was, 'Do you know how much money you are worth?' Except I didn't take it as a compliment – I hated him when he told me that, especially when he had a sly smile on his face.

The trouble was, I most definitely was worth a hell of a lot of money to Peter. Little innocent, angelic-looking me, with my short, tousled brown hair, slim body, full lips and soft round eyes – well, I was every perverted man's dream.

When I was eight, those film afternoons turned into a whole lot more than just watching cartoons and witnessing a naked two-year-old race around the living room sporting an erection. That was when Peter's friends and colleagues paid for me to take part in 'anal rimming', a degrading but very popular practice in his circle.

Peter fed me so much sweet stuff and chocolate in order

for the sugars to seep through my skin in my sweat and give off quite a unique smell, which some men apparently found very stimulating.

There were specific men who paid Peter to take me to a place where they wouldn't be disturbed – often the room at the Freemason's hall, which Peter kept close tabs on, and which he had the key for at all times. The room had to be very warm and I would be forced to lie face down on a bed or a chair, showing my bare bottom. I always took this to mean that the men didn't want to see my face – maybe it was a reminder that they were doing something very wrong.

Often they licked my bottom and the soles of my feet. Some of them loved to play with my little toes, sucking each of them one by one as they masturbated. And there were others who wanted to push their penises between my feet, which led to a very quick orgasm spilling semen all over my toes. I hated it – the smell and the stickiness made me gag as Peter wiped it off later with a dirty rag. I always made sure I had a long soak in the bath later to get rid of all traces of those men.

It was during those times on my own in the bath or in bed that I wondered if this was what happened to other children. Were other kids forced to do unspeakable and disgusting things to older men? Did they spend their days dreading the sound of their father's car door because it meant he was home and probably wanted something from them? How did other children spend their play-time? Was this what a childhood really was about or was there something better out there for me? And if this

wasn't a normal childhood, would I ever be rescued from my prison?

Looking back, I didn't have a childhood after I turned five and became useful to Peter. The bedtime stories about princesses and horses were over, I wasn't tucked into my bed any more and my parents, the only constants in my life, never told me that they loved me. I lacked everything that a childhood should have in it – loving parents, a safe environment, a happy and innocent existence, friends to play with and, above all, being told that, no matter what, I was protected and I always would be.

The only kind of gratitude for my existence came from the men I serviced for Peter. The men were always very nice to me, bringing me small chocolates and a few special sweets from the local shop, or sometimes even small items of clothing, like a cute little skirt or a fancy T-shirt. Every-one who was a regular knew how much I loved horses, so there was never any shortage of horse books with pictures, or plastic horses.

I was always told that I was the most beautiful girl that they had ever seen but, inside, I always felt that this wasn't true. I knew that men liked the princess type, with long blonde, curly hair, perfect porcelain skin and big blue doe eyes. I often got to see some of the other girls who were pimped out when I was taken to meet the men and this was typically how most of them looked. But I realised that I had a staggering presence about me and I knew that because Peter was always telling me how my 'uncles' loved me so much, that they kept coming back to see me.

The men remembered me not so much for my looks but

for my innocence and the way in which I managed to keep that. I could have become a completely different girl, I know, but somehow I retained that air of innocence, as if I was fresh on the scene and had never been touched by another man. This was something that all the perverts liked about me, especially when they were filming me. On screen I was a sweet little girl who all the viewers, in their fantasies, desperately wanted to meet in real life.

Peter let this sick abuse carry on until I was about 10 and, by then, it was as common an occurrence for me as going to school. I still can't believe that I can say that – it's such an awful thing to remember and to know that the innocent child that I was did not know it was wrong.

When I turned 10, Peter allowed his clients to perform anal sex on me, and I am guessing that it was more lucrative for him money-wise because I remember I was very busy being ferried here, there and everywhere to people's houses or to the Freemason's hall. Peter was always sneaking me out under some pretence or other, telling Christine all sorts of lies to get me out of the house.

I remember the first man who paid for anal sex with me had a small penis, much smaller than I was used to seeing. I think he was of Japanese or Chinese origin and I remember being fascinated by his tiny black eyes and the difference in their shape. He smelled very different to other men. Unlike the usual Old Spice sort of aftershaves that the other men used to bathe themselves in, he reeked of tea and biscuits and, unlike my other 'uncles', he wouldn't look me in the eye at all. He was very quietly spoken. 'This might be painful,' he said, his voice low. 'You might even faint

with the pain.' I was still too young for full anal penetration and, although I didn't know it at the time, this was
going to be my training day.

He leaned down and tried to kiss my anus and, as I felt
his tongue, I winced and pulled away – I couldn't help it, it
felt so strange. 'What is he going to do next?' I thought, as
I wished I could get out of that room as quickly as possible.
I knew it was going to be horrible as he unbuttoned his
trousers and pulled out his tiny but erect penis. He rubbed
himself against me and I winced again, so he spat on his
fingers and used them to penetrate me slightly. I jumped
upright – it was like having a hot needle moved around
inside me.

I started to cry but he didn't hear – he was having too
much of a good time. Luckily for me, it was all over in a
minute and a half and, after he had pulled his trousers up,
he left me on the carpet like a piece of meat. Everything
seemed hot to me – the carpet, my rear end, even my face
felt like it was burning.

Peter came into the room then. 'Go to the toilet and
peewee,' he said. 'All the funny stuff will drop out. Try and
have a poo as well if you can. It will help.'

I sat on the toilet and screamed, tears sizzling on my
cheeks. 'I can't go, I can't go,' I cried. 'Everything hurts. It's
sore. The peewee is burning me too!'

Peter gave me a toothbrush cup filled with warm water
and a little bit of disinfectant. 'Rinse your bottom,' he
ordered. 'You'll be fine. Stop crying.'

The hospital smell I associated with the disinfectant was
a comfort to me because I knew that it would make me

better. I had no idea that I had suffered minor rectal trauma that day, nor did I have a clue that years of doing this would lead to future health problems for me. I was just content to be clean again. I didn't speak much at all on the way back to the house that I called my 'home'. I was still in shock, I think.

Soon after, Peter educated me in simple terms about a man's anatomy and the favourite places where he liked to be touched. I remember he sat me down in my bedroom one afternoon when I got home from school, a sure sign that something was going to happen. I had got used to these little 'chats' and had long known never to repeat any of them to Christine or anyone else. I knew that, if I did, I would suffer badly.

'There is a special little place in a man's bum that, when they cum and they grunt, the place inside their body stretches and puts pressure on a little thing around it called the prostate,' Peter told me. 'If you can touch their bums nicely, you could help a man to have the best possible orgasm that they can ever have and they will be very happy.'

Yes, and looking back, I am sure that Peter was very happy too, since he could charge extra for those perks.

I was instructed on how to make his clients happy. I had to concentrate on touching their arseholes while they licked my boobs, which were very slow in forming, but I guess the little buds were enough to give them a lot of pleasure.

I would move my fingers around inside the men and often I would feel them squeeze their back passage around

them as they groaned or squealed. I quickly caught on that, by stimulating the man's anal prostate, it led to a very quick orgasm and less work for me.

A year or so after my anal-sex education, Peter allowed me to start using fruits, like bananas, and veggies when servicing his clients. Before that, however, we had to practise together, and the fun for Peter was to see the banana going into me.

This practice of anal insertion was also a favourite of Peter's. He loved inserting foreign objects up himself for sexual pleasure and he would often try them out on me first to see if they were easy to use. He would gently push small glass tubes or vials into my bottom to see what would happen. I would have to lie there very still while he did so, the added danger being that, if I resisted or moved, it could crack either inside me or around my anus.

The list of objects would continue to grow and he would taunt me when the excitement of his plans got too much for him. That's when he would have to find a quick, safe place where he could ejaculate quickly – I lost count of the number of times he drove us to a remote park or car park so that I could help him to orgasm.

In the car, he would push my head into his lap where his erect penis would be waiting. 'Suck on this – you see what you've made me do?' he would snarl, trying to control his excitement.

He would gasp and growl and throw his red face back with the pleasure he was feeling. Breathing heavily like he was going to have a heart attack, he would finish ejaculating all over me and the car seat and then wipe up

with the handkerchiefs and the tissues that he had stashed in the car ready for moments such as those.

We would then drive home as if nothing had happened. Sick. I was always so glad to get home. I'd go straight to the bathroom to scrub my teeth to get rid of the taste. Often, I would scrub so hard that my gums bled but at least I felt clean again as I rid myself of his poison.

Peter had always made a big thing of my virginity being intact and there was a major reason for this. The fact that he had in his possession a whole little girl with a perfect rosebud waiting to be picked by the 'right person' for the 'right reasons' was a great selling point.

He would often get calls from his clients asking for a virgin girl and he would do his best to go out there and find one. Of course, virgin girls were much more expensive than a 'used' girl, since they were considered a rare commodity and purer. Peter had such a big network of paedophiles with access to girls and boys of all ages that all it took was a phone call to find a virgin and that same day there she was, all ready to be used and abused.

Where I was concerned though, I was all Peter's and, probably from the moment he met me, I was borne, he had decided that, as his property, he was going to be the man to take my virginity. As the head of the family and as the man who pretty much owned every move I made, he assumed he had the right to take whatever he wanted from me and he had the monumental day all planned out.

Peter had been watching and waiting for the time when he could have the house to himself and, therefore, have plenty of time to savour the event.

The intimate, warm, custard-like spot hidden very deep inside my body, nearest the very soul of me, was about to be ripped to the outside world by a man who cared very little for me as a person. Although I don't doubt Peter had some feelings for me, instead of being my father, he was my keeper and, as such, he had the right – in his mind – to do whatever he wanted with me.

The day eventually came when I was 13 years old. It was a clear day and it was lovely and warm. Christine had decided to take Tracy out for her appointment at the doctor's, where they were to evaluate her for improvement on her condition. The doctor was a specialist paediatrician and she had a reputation for showing remarkable accuracy and compassion in dealing with children who had problems similar to Tracy's.

I remember the two blondes – inseparable as always – started to get their stuff together to leave the house. Christine seemed excited and hopeful, something I hadn't seen in her for a long time. She had a bounce in her step, as she believed that the doctor was finally going to diagnose her little angel. I sometimes don't think she cared what exactly was wrong with Tracy as long as she had answers to her burning questions. Nothing else mattered to her; she was totally focused on getting some much-needed help for her daughter.

They left without a nod in my direction, which was normal. Christine rarely even acknowledged me in those days, unless, of course, she wanted me to do something like the cleaning or helping out with Tracy. Then she would be full on, screaming my name, telling me what to do, rather than asking me nicely.

The traditional rituals of a hospital appointment seemed different that morning. I could feel it in my soul. And I was right. It was very different.

My breakfast was on the side waiting for me in the kitchen and so was my large cup of tea with milk and three sugars. The bathroom door was closed from the inside and that was unusual – Peter being in the bathroom with the door closed. When Christine wasn't around, he left it open, as we had such intimate knowledge of each other's bodies and personal toilet habits that a closed bathroom door made very little difference between us.

The biggest change to the day was that Peter had showered and shaved. He had prepared himself as a man would on his wedding day, one of the biggest and most personal days of a man's life. He was ready to take my virginity. I just didn't know it.

Peter took the shaving lotion off the shelf – the lotion reserved for special days and holidays, anniversary, birthdays and Christmas, even Easter time. He splashed on a little to smell nice before he walked into the kitchen while I was eating my toast and jam. 'Can I have a bit?' he asked, smiling. I gave him the toast without question and he took a bite before giving it back to me.

He was different that day – kinder and more thoughtful. The stern, bleak eyes that would normally bore holes into me if I did something wrong were not there. He had a much softer look about him and I could feel that the energy coming from him was different. He touched my back, tracing my spine without saying a word, and then he left the kitchen to head towards his bedroom.

When I went upstairs, I saw that Peter was still in his dressing gown and his slippers. I had my gown on too and my slippers, as I wasn't asked to rush to get dressed. We were not going out early anyway and I sauntered into my bedroom, absolutely sure that Peter would come in for something. It was rare that I was left alone when there were just the two of us in the house – he always wanted me for something.

I loved my bedroom. It had been fitted with mirrors so that, as I approached my teenage years, I could dress and pose, do my hair and spend ages looking at different outfits, just like a normal kid of that age. I also had a small dressing table where I displayed my own perfumes that I had started to collect.

Peter suddenly, and not surprisingly, walked through the door. Of course, he didn't knock or ask if he could come, he just opened the door and walked right in. I was choosing clothes to get changed into as he walked past me and sat on my bed. He held a package in his hands. He motioned to me to sit with him.

I did as he wanted and he gave me the package. 'These are for you, the very first. They're in white. You can wear them straight away and I hope you like them,' he said in a soft voice. I just stared at the package because I had no idea what he was giving me. 'Well, open it then!' he said excitedly.

'A present in the middle of the week,' I thought as I pulled open the brown paper. 'That's weird.' I was cautious though, because gifts meant different things to me. A gift was usually a 'payment' for being a good girl to one of the

many men he was pimping me out to, or he had a special 'uncle' that he wanted me to service later or on the weekend, and it was Peter's way of softening the request.

As I took the package, I noticed the all-too-familiar bulge under his dressing gown. Peter was fidgeting and that was unusual for him. In fact, he seemed rather on edge. He was acting as if something was important and different. I definitely felt as if something was different – the frostiness had gone. He was acting like I was more of an equal and I felt that he wanted me to like him.

I tore open the package to find a pretty little training bra, a little padded and decorated with lace and bows. It had thick straps to offer support and, even though I didn't have much there to fill it, I was thrilled and excited. All of my friends at school were wearing bras and, whenever I had asked Christine for one, she had taunted me that I didn't need one.

I pulled off my dressing gown and, with one flourish, held the bra up to my chest and pranced around the room with it in front of me. 'How does it look, Dad,' I asked as I twirled around. 'Can you help me to put in on, please?'

Peter pulled me over and showed me how to adjust the straps and then he clasped it at my back. He then turned it around and carefully pulled the straps up over my arms and adjusted them to size. The bra felt scratchy and I felt like there was a band around my body holding in my breath.

'It's so tight. Why is it so tight?' I asked. 'Is it supposed to be tight like that? 'I looked up and quizzed him, expecting an immediate answer. I forgot that, as a man, he

didn't wear a bra and wouldn't know if it was meant to be tight or not.

I fiddled around to make my small breasts comfortable in the new training bra. I looked into the mirror and pranced like a show pony in front of it, all the time watching Peter and expecting some sort of response from him. But he remained silent.

The breeze outside the window became obvious as the room was so quiet, and I became quiet too. Half-naked, I turned completely to face Peter and he asked me to sit on the bed near to him.

He lay back and asked me to sit on top of him as if I was riding a horse. This was not an unusual request – one of my favourite games with Peter had been when he bounced me up and down when I was younger.

I jumped up onto him with my new training bra in place. I sat on top of his dressing gown and began chattering about the bra but Peter wasn't listening – he was playing out his master plan in his head, following years of planning.

He grabbed my hips and whispered, 'Now, what will happen may sting a bit at first but then it will be fine. All right?' I didn't have a clue what he meant, so I wasn't prepared for what was going to happen next.

He slipped his hand down my knickers and began to rub me. Knowing what Peter was usually after, I took his penis in my hands and moved my mouth towards it. But he pulled away from me.

'Not that way today.'

I looked at him, bemused, and I let go of him. 'Come

and sit on me again. This may sting just a little. You will be a woman.'

I was only 13 years old – I didn't understand what he meant by 'being a woman'.

Peter wet his hand and shoved it back down my knickers. He pushed my back down on the bed and then moved me up onto his chest with one motion, so that my breasts, hidden by my new training bra, pushed against his hairless chest. Then he carefully spread my legs open wide as he helped direct his quivering penis into my vagina.

I winced as the tearing feeling began inside and I began to burn and sting. He felt so very big as he slowly pushed his penis deeper into my small hole. There was enormous pressure down there and I felt as though my insides were bending with the force. I tried to sit up but he pushed me down, demanding that I keep still.

'Don't move,' he said. 'Then it won't hurt so much. Just keep still.' I remember he sounded almost panicky. 'Just keep fucking still, will you?'

I could tell by his tone that, if I didn't comply, I would be in masses of trouble, so I lay back down on his chest and kept still.

He was close to ejaculation as I felt him to see just how far he was buried inside my soul. As I touched his penis, he gave one huge push and screamed out, 'Yes, oh, yes! Now you belong to me. You're all mine, you're mine now.' He pushed again. 'Fuck, what a warm, sweet little cunt you have! What a good girl you are.' He told me that 'fucking me' that day gave him the best orgasm of his entire life, as if that was meant to make me feel any better.

I was too stunned to speak, smeared as I was in blood and other bodily fluids. I felt disgusting inside and out. I wanted to run away as fast as I could and never, ever see Peter's face again. I knew that what had happened was wrong but I was trapped. I had no one to turn to. I felt lost.

Peter was obviously proud of what he had achieved that morning. After all, taking my virginity was an event that he had built up in his sordid mind for years and I guess, by all accounts, it was possibly the best experience of his depraved sexual life. Under his breath, he said to himself, 'Fuck, that was good.'

He picked me up and he told me to go to the bathroom to get cleaned up before he lit a cigarette and sat back in the chair like the cat that got the cream. My God, he was so obviously chuffed with himself.

I went to the bathroom and my knees were shaking so badly that I thought I might collapse. I sat on the toilet and my whole body started to shake, as if I was freezing – of course, it was the shock. I was burning inside and, as I sat to pee, it felt like a million razor blades were slicing my private areas all at once.

I grabbed the shaving mirror and took a look at myself. My parts were rather swollen, which hammered home the horrific truth of what had just happened. I was no longer a virgin and, even though I had suffered countless other sexual acts on my body, this was somehow the worst.

I caught my breath as the stinging continued and I grabbed a face cloth to wipe away the sticky residue that was left on my private parts. As I staggered back into my bedroom and threw myself on my bed into the foetal

position, I felt absolute terror and shame. I didn't feel like a beautiful girl at all, not a supposed 'woman' in any way. More like half a person.

Almost insane with grief over what had happened to me, I started the long path to heal within myself. To do this, I made a vow that I would not allow myself to show any of the emotions that I was going through. I would not give Peter the pleasure of seeing how I felt and I wouldn't ever show emotion when I was with his clients. It was the only coping mechanism that would save me. That day, a dark corner had been turned and any scrap of innocence that had been left in me was gone.

I pretended that I had pains so that I could stay in my bed and Peter let me as he went outside to mow the lawn. I felt so alone as I lay there. The bed that had once been my safe haven, where I would lie and read my horsey books at night, was now, and would continue to be, a constant reminder of the day he took what was sacred to me.

So I could never say I lost my virginity, as I didn't lose it – it was not lost at all. I knew who had it and where it was. Peter had stolen the last piece of me that had been sacred and untouched by a human being. I lay there and sobbed until the bed-sheets that I hugged around my body up to my neck were damp with tears.

I was still in bed when Christine and Tracy returned from their appointment. Peter had told her that I had gone back to bed with a cold, so she popped her head round the door to offer me some aspirin and orange juice to ward off my symptoms. I didn't say anything – I knew better than to tell Christine my latest secret.

As I lay there thinking about what had just happened, I wished with all of my heart that I hadn't been submissive and let Peter do what he had wanted to. If only I'd had the courage to stand up to him, to tell him to take his hands off me, to tell him that I didn't want all those perverts touching me. If only, if only, *if only* I'd had the courage to stop it all when it had started and tell someone what was going on. Yet it wasn't as simple as that. I had no one to turn to and I knew that Peter would hurt me if I didn't comply – the fear was always deep inside of me and I don't think it ever left me.

The loss of my virginity to Peter was an event that would be in all my dreams for the remainder of my life, haunting me and reminding me of what a spineless wimp I'd been, alone without a friend in the world, reminding me I never did anything to stop him taking my honour. Peter left me with a hollow feeling inside just at the top of my stomach.

Unfortunately for me, after my virginity was gone, I was no longer a prize that wasn't to be touched by anyone else and I was, therefore, ready to be pimped out for regular sex, rather than just the anal variety I was popular for.

Once I remembered my past, it was a day I never forgot again.

CHAPTER FIVE

CHILD
PORN STAR

Peter used his job as a way of setting up meetings for people to have sex with me. He would arrange a time to go to a client's house to lay a floor. In those days the tiles were stuck down on the kitchen floor with very strong, foul-smelling glue, so Peter always advised the wife and children to vacate the house for a few hours until the smell died down. As soon as they were gone and the house was empty, Peter would leave and the man of the house would have sex with me, although never vaginal sex because that little part of me was reserved solely for Peter's pleasure.

I often thought of escape when I was lying in bed at night or gazing out of the window in a dream. Anything had to be better than the life I was being forced to lead but where on earth would I go to and how would I get there? What would I do for money? I knew that Peter would find me for sure because he had so many contacts everywhere –

there would be no hiding place for me. Lord, how I hated everything about him and I hated Christine almost as much because she was oblivious to what was going on. I couldn't believe that the person who I thought to be my mother didn't see what her own husband was doing to her child. Either she did have an inkling, or she was in denial, or she knew all along and chose not to step in and stop it all. I didn't have a clue which of these it was but, whatever, I blamed her for what my life had turned into.

Peter, ever the snake, was relentless in finding ways to make more money out of me, but by the same token he was careful not to alert anyone to what was happening. At one point he seemed to be tired of setting me up with different men, of driving me out to meet them and having to wait while they took advantage of me. I'm not sure whether the excitement of it all was disappearing or if it had become a chore, or even if he was worried about getting caught. I felt that he was looking for different ways in which to exploit me. Regardless of how bored he was getting with it all, I was making money and that's what made his world go around.

I'm still unsure about the number of 'uncles' who sexually abused me. I believe that in the space of a year I was raped by more than 60 different men. At the same time, Peter was raping me whenever he felt the urge. He would force me to give him oral sex, usually in the back of the car, parked up behind trees in a local beauty spot, or he would make me wank him off while he was at home. Sometimes he would have me wash myself in the bath and, as he stood there watching, he would masturbate. I

wonder if Christine and Peter had a sex life or not, and perhaps a lack of passion in their own relationship was a big reason why he used me so often. Certainly after Tracy was born, Christine had turned into a homely sort in her apron and comfortable shoes – a bit of a change from the high heels and good times that they enjoyed when they were courting and newly married. I don't think Christine would have had the energy or the desire to fulfil Peter's sexual needs either, because her days of looking after Tracy were long and tiring.

Every night I made sure that I had a bath and it had to be scalding hot to the point where I would get out and I would be like a boiled lobster. Once in there, I would spend 20 minutes scrubbing my body with a sponge or a brush in a vain attempt to rid myself of the smells of the men who I had been forced upon that day, and the shameful acts that I had been made to take part in. It was only when I felt completely cleansed that I would get out, pull on my dressing gown, and to go to bed. Sometimes I made my skin bleed because I had scrubbed so hard and it left little scabs that Peter would put antiseptic cream on, so that they would disappear quickly and wouldn't put his clients off when they saw my body.

I was raped so many times that, just like the anal sex, it became a normal way of life for me. To ensure that I didn't get pregnant by him, Peter even took me to the doctors to get the contraceptive pill on the grounds that I was suffering from acne. He had heard that the pill with its different hormones can help a woman suffering from acne and as I did have some spots on my face and back, it was

the best cover to have a doctor prescribe it to me. Of course, the doctor didn't imagine that it was because I was having regular sex otherwise I am certain I wouldn't have got it. Peter thought of absolutely everything – he was quite the genius in covering his tracks and thwarting suspicion of any kind. I know that I became a much different child; a withdrawn teenager who lived for the times when I could go to the stables and spend time with the horses. Those were the only occasions when I felt safe and I allowed myself to cry my heart out to my horse, to let my guard down and release all the unhappiness and torment that had flooded my entire life.

Peter also started taking me to paedophile parties that were organised by his network of members. These parties were often much bigger, with dozens of men being involved, and I hated them. More men made me more afraid but, on the rare occasions when I refused to go with him, Peter would fly into a rage and hit the table with his fist, especially if Christine wasn't there to witness his anger. My food and drink would go flying and the look on his face was so evil that it was like looking at the devil himself. Then I would be so desperately afraid that I would go along with him without saying another word. Looking back, I don't know if I was afraid of getting a beating or terrified that Peter would kill me if I didn't comply. Whatever it was, he had such a hold over me and every aspect of my life that I felt as if I was in a prison without bars.

Peter was also very much in on the action of organising parties. There was a network of safe homes across a large

area and many of these places had cellars and outbuildings, just private and big enough to be able to invite enough people to make it worthwhile. There were farms, barns, bed-and-breakfasts and a guest house with a kitchen in the cellar area where he would hold the illegal parties. He was able to charge a fee for attendance and, when he had the man there to film the atrocities, Peter was then able to sell or hire the film afterwards to those who wanted to continue the pleasure. I didn't see any point in it at all. I couldn't understand why the men wanted to see the whole set of events over and over again, when it was nothing like being at the actual event itself. Maybe for memories – who the hell knows what really went on in their perverted, twisted minds? I didn't realise until much later on in my life that the men were able to imagine what it was like and also look at what the others had done and then, perhaps, if that specific child was available the next time, they could request or choose that child themselves. Also it meant that they were able to masturbate to the film in peace and in private. To this day I worry that a child porn film will surface on a digitally remastered DVD, with me in it as the star. It may sound an extreme thing to worry about but there's every chance one could turn up some day – I don't know what I would do if it did.

Another memory I had repressed until the bang on my head during the Tube bombing, was my fear of dogs. Anything larger than a miniature schnauzer or a cocker spaniel coming towards me in the park or the street brought about a deep fear that would make me turn the other way. My heart would start to pound with such

ferocity that I struggled to breath and I would sweat until I was well out of the way.

Before the bombing, I could never understand why I would have such a reaction in the pit of my stomach whenever I even so much as thought about a big dog or saw one on the TV. I had never been attacked by a large dog, nor had I ever had a bad experience with one. In fact, I don't think a big dog had even growled at me or shown me its teeth, as far as I was aware.

However, after 7 July 2005 the memories came back clearly. I recalled an out-of-the-way sort of place, in an underground cellar, which could have been in a guest house or a private home. Wherever it was, it was certainly a place that was big enough to house a group of men and have them park their cars or travel by taxi without causing suspicion. The place was dimly lit. There were cages that housed dogs of various sizes and I remember that some were large black-and-white Great Danes. I also noticed two cages housing a Labrador and a Staffordshire Terrier. The Staffie was a bulky little boy, a caramel colour, short in stature, and he had a smiling face, so I took to him right away. It looked like he had been in a few dog fights because there were some cuts, scrapes and numerous scars on his chunky body.

When we arrived, Peter was holding my hand in the darkness until our eyes grew accustomed to the murkiness. He had spoken to a chap who was arranging comfortable chairs and he had also brought the kitchen chairs down to an area on the carpet and arranged them into a circle. There was a long deep-pile soft rug in the middle of the

room. I noticed a big bowl of water on the side and, across the room, a bucket of warm water. The dogs were barking at each other and some were getting aggressive and wanted to fight. One of the smaller dogs was in the corner of his cage. His name was Pepe and he was the cutest little dog – a ball of white fluff. I remember thinking how silly he was to hurt himself like that. At this point. I hadn't got a clue about what was going to happen – it was all new to me.

The respective dog owners covered the cages with thick blankets and the dogs became calmer and quietened down. 'Would you like to see Pepe?' his owner asked me, and I was excited.

'Yes please, sir,' I said and he opened the cage door so that Pepe could walk out. He came straight to me, tail wagging furiously, obviously so happy to see a friendly face. Pepe licked me as I crouched down to speak to him – he was such a sweet little boy, obviously starved of love and affection. He didn't want to leave me when his owner dragged him by his collar and lead and gave him to another man to hold. I wanted to hold him, to spend more time with him, but I didn't dare ask. It was quite obvious to me that something major was going to happen. Pepe's owner gave me a facecloth to wipe his slobber off my legs but what I didn't see in the dimly lit room was that the face cloth had a lot of blood on it, along with excretions from a female dog, who was in season and ready to be mated.

Suddenly, Pepe became very interested in my leg and he started to lick it, then he started to hump it. I thought it was rather funny at first, not associating the flannel and what was on the piece of material with any of this. The

room was getting hot and I had a small jumper on, which I took off as everyone filed in rather quietly. Peter had told me to take it off because he said that it was going to get very hot in that room and that the men wanted to see my figure. There were other girls there too, including a drunken teenage girl who was still drinking and getting drunker by the minute.

The men had created a ring in the middle of the room and some already had a tell-tale bulge in their pants, so I knew something of a sexual nature was going to happen. They stood there with their hands in their pockets, trying to conceal their erections, waiting to find out what the 'floor show' would be that evening. I wondered if there was going to be some dog fighting, considering all the animals that were also in the room.

A young girl, who was also a bit drunk, was brought down the stairs and placed in one of the comfy chairs, where she was plied with more alcohol – I think she was given a beer and some wine to drink. She was very wobbly and giggled with a slurred tone. More men started to arrive and what seemed like a few minutes later the room was packed to the gills with people waiting to see the evening's entertainment.

The drunk teenager, a couple of other girls and I were led to the middle of the room in front of everyone, where we were stripped of our bottom underwear and left with just our vests on. The drunk girl just kept her bra on. We were in candlelight and there was faint music from a radio, which sounded scratchy as the station signal got lost every now and then. I looked at Peter and he smiled that slimy

over me. I got up and ran into the corner of the room as Pepe was led back to his cage.

I didn't know what to do so Peter came over and gathered me up and told me to wash up. 'You were a very good girl tonight,' he said with a smile. 'You did really well for your first time.' I was beyond humiliated. If I could have died right there and then, I would happily have done so. It was one of the worst experiences Peter had ever subjected me to and I wanted to hit out, to scream, to cry and to run out of that room that stunk of stale cigarettes and bodily fluids. I felt more disgusted with myself than I had ever been before in my life. Part of me couldn't believe the depravity of what had just happened and I couldn't understand why they got their kicks out of watching humans and animals doing it together. I had never imagined that there was something like cross-species mating – it seemed like the dirtiest thing in the world right then, and something that was completely unnatural.

I was quiet that night going home in the car. Peter had a bulge in his pocket, only this time it was a bulge created by the roll of hundreds of bank notes – the takings from the evening's illegal entertainment. He was very chirpy but I couldn't even look at him without crying. I didn't want to talk to him, I didn't want him near me, I didn't want any-thing to do with him. When we got back home, he told Christine that he had won the 'darts contest' and had the winnings in cash to prove it. 'It was a great game – we slaughtered the opposition,' he said, laughing as Christine counted all the money from his pocket.

'Wow,' she said. 'You did do well, Peter. That's amazing.'

She gave him a long kiss on his lips, a sure sign of her approval and, no doubt, she was already thinking about what she was going to spend that money on.

Through this bestiality, Peter had found his new avenue to make money and the huge financial rewards far surpassed anything he had been dabbling in up until then. I don't like to even think about the other times I was forced to have sex with a dog – there were too many to count and the memories are incredibly painful and degrading even now. I know that it happened often enough for a great deal of money to be made, enough to buy two new cars outright, both the same colour in midnight blue, with matching 'His' and 'Hers' signs painted in gold on the back of each of the boots.

CHAPTER SIX

HUMBUG, MY FOUR-LEGGED SAVIOUR

As Peter's abuse of me escalated, I had to find my own coping mechanism. I'm not sure I would be around today otherwise. I think I'd have run away and also got into some kind of trouble with drugs, or I'd maybe even have hurt myself to escape the emotional and physical pain.

The horrors that I endured at his hands were the stuff of your very worst nightmares and I had to find my place where I could switch off from it all and become a kid again. I had to find a place where nobody was in a position to be allowed to abuse me and where I was in control.

That sanctuary was the stables where I learned to ride.

A lady called Joan owned the stables. She was in her early thirties and had once been a successful dressage rider. What she didn't know about looking after horses and riding them wasn't worth knowing at all.

I liked her because she was very much of the view that, no matter what your background, if you had talent and you worked hard, you could be whatever you wanted to be. She fuelled my dreams of being a horse rider and she taught me that the hard work she preached really could make a difference.

When I was nine, I was riding quite proficiently every Saturday morning, but I wanted more. I wanted to stay all day with the horses and help out at the yard with Joan and all the other young riders who gave their time to feed, muck out stables and help the little kids get their horses ready.

Christine had no problem with me going to the stables for the whole day. That way, I was out of her hair and she was with her precious Tracy. I was such an inconvenience for her once Tracy came along, so the chance to get rid of me for the whole day was something she jumped at. Besides, as I grew older, the stables became a bargaining tool for her.

'If you don't want to be bothered doing the dishes, you won't be going to the stables,' she would threaten me. I had very few friends and I never had sleepovers, so she couldn't have held that against me. The only thing in my life that I cherished was my Saturdays at the barn – and Christine knew that only too well. I would quickly back down and be compliant because the chance that I might not go to the stables was absolutely unthinkable.

I remember she knitted me a thick sweater for the cold weather and on a Saturday morning she would make a packed lunch consisting of a ham sandwich, crisps, a piece

of cake and sometimes an item of fruit. She would also pack me a beaker of juice or send me off with a cup of tea to keep me warm if it was chilly.

Peter would drop me off and for the whole day I would be among kids my own age – some older kids too – and I was with my equine friends. To me, I was in my own piece of heaven right there. I loved cleaning stalls, grooming the horses, putting their tack on, leading them out for the little kids, then giving them their dinner at night just before Peter picked me up to go home. I didn't mind that I went home every Saturday with poop on my boots and stinking like a horse – I loved everything that was part of life around horses.

By the time I was 10, I was trusted by Joan to get the animals ready for the rich kids who owned them and kept them there, and I got paid for that. It wasn't a lot of money but it was enough for me to save up to buy knee-length riding boots, more modern jodhpurs and a nice navy jacket instead of having to wear the ugly olive-green quilted one that Christine had bought me from the second-hand store.

This money was always my money. Christine and Peter never asked for it, and having that bit of pocket money meant that I never asked them for anything, so I guess it was more advantageous for them to let me keep the little bit of cash I earned from Joan. Earning my own money did wonders for my self-esteem, which was really low because of the abuse. It gave me the hope that one day I might have enough money to go off on my own, away from Christine and Peter, to somewhere far away where I would never be touched by another man again.

When I was 12, Joan wanted some work doing to increase the number of stalls at the stables and, as she knew that Peter was a dab hand at construction work, she asked him to come to the property, take a look and give her a price for the work. She already had a really nice area with 12 big stalls, but she was thinking of expanding her business. The stables were always busy with the children who came for lessons and, as her reputation was growing, so were the requests from rich people wanting to keep their prized horses at her facility.

Peter came up with an idea that he would build the 12 stalls on the back of the others, as this would save Joan a lot of money and space. I wasn't particularly thrilled that he had been asked to do the job, because it meant that, instead of dropping me off at the stables, he would be there for most of the day with his builders, working.

But then I had what I considered to be a brainwave. If Joan had a spare stall, maybe I could have a horse of my own. 'Are you expecting the new barn to be full?' I asked her.

'Well, there will be a few new ones but there might be one or two stalls spare. Why?' she said.

I think that she knew what I was getting at but I didn't mention a horse to her and, even though I'd dropped hints to Peter, he always seemed to dismiss them, as did Christine, if I ever said dreamily that I wanted my own horse.

Once the stables were finished, we had a little painting party to paint them all white and they looked fantastic. That same day there was a lot of excitement around the

stables. 'Did you see the new black horse?' one of the girls asked me. 'Joan has a new horse and he looks very nice.' A few of us made our way to the riding field and there was Joan sitting on a rather large black horse that it looked like she was trying to control. On the ground was a selection of bits – these metal pieces fit in the mouth and, when you pull on them with the reins, the bit helps to control the horse – and I think she was trying them all out to see which was best to use with this particular horse.

I remember the gelding was dripping in sweat as it took her a good 20 minutes to have him under her control but, after that, he behaved very nicely considering he had only just arrived in new surroundings and wasn't familiar with anything or anybody. The horse had once been a driving pony, which accounted for his 'hard' mouth, which wasn't very sensitive to the bit when Joan pulled on the reins.

Once she had finished, Joan turned to me. 'Can you take the new pony and give him a good bath?' she asked. 'He needs tidying up a bit too – he's a bit overgrown around the face and tail!' I was only too happy to be the one who was entrusted with the care of the new horse and I took my time with him. I cut the whiskers gently from his muzzle, I trimmed his thick tail, which was dragging on the ground, and I groomed him until he gleamed in the sunshine.

I was already falling for him. He had a kind eye and he obviously loved the attention he was getting. He didn't fight the hose or the shampoo and, when I got close to his head, he put it down to my level so that I could brush his pretty face and comb his long forelock. After at least an hour of beauty treatment, I led him back

to his new stall, almost at the end of the new row of stalls that Peter had built.

'You need to give him a name,' Joan said, and I remember thinking, 'Why are you asking me?'

A little crowd of kids had gathered at the stall and Peter stopped what he was doing and came over too.

'You need to think of a name for him, Beverli,' Joan said again and she was beaming. 'Your dad has built all these stables and done all the roofing so that you can have this horse. He's your horse now, Beverli.'

I couldn't speak. Peter was looking at me with a sly smile on his face and the rest of the girls were beside themselves with excitement for me. It was such an incredible shock because never in a million years did I ever think I would be lucky enough to get my own pony. In those days, horse riding was something the rich kids did and, although Peter earned good money, I didn't think we could afford this. But Joan gave us the stable for nothing because Peter was always on hand to do her odd jobs around the barn – it must have been an agreement they'd made before they found me my horse, whom I christened Humbug – or Hummy for short. I used my wages from Joan to pay for the straw and his feed and that was all that I needed money-wise to pay for him because I earned all my lessons.

Humbug cost £80 and Peter had bought him from an old man who had used him as a driving pony more than for anything else. Sadly, the old man had become ill and couldn't look after him anymore, so he wanted to sell him to a good home. I think that Joan heard about him on the grapevine and thought he would be a good match for me,

but I still don't know if she approached Peter with the idea of me having a horse, or if he had brought it up with her. Either way, I was the happiest girl in the world that day. My own horse! A real-life, stomping, breathing horse who was all mine. It was something I had prayed for as long as I could remember. I was just completely elated that our paths had crossed and I knew that we would be good together. I couldn't wait to get on him but we decided to leave that first ride for the next day so that he would have the chance to completely settle down.

I had to be dragged home that night. All I wanted to do was to be with Humbug. I remember I got home and counted down the hours until the next day when I would see him again and hopefully ride him. It was arranged that during school days Joan would feed him in the morning and turn him out into the field, then after school Peter would take me to the barn so that I could ride him, muck him out and feed him.

It was a lot of work and part of me was a bit surprised that Peter had agreed to it all. He had always had such total control over me and where I was going or who I was with and then, suddenly, he was allowing me to spend a lot of extra time away from him with people my own age. For a long time it didn't make sense, until much later when I sat down and worked it all out.

Everybody liked Peter and he loved the feeling that he was revered by seemingly everyone he met. He had already gained a reputation at the barn as the nice dad who did all of Joan's little jobs for nothing; the good guy who dropped everything to help out when he could. So many people

would say to me, 'You're so lucky – your dad is such a diamond,' meaning how nice he was to everyone.

I believe, by helping Joan out such a lot, it was not only a good boost to his ego but a way that he could make amends in his own mind for the wicked things he was doing to me and to other young girls with his perverted friends. I think, in his mind, he thought that if he could help others out as much as he could, it was offsetting all the horrific abuse and, therefore, his conscience was always clear.

And I also think that having me at the stables all day Saturday was a very safe place for him. At the stables, parents were always coming and going dropping their kids off – there was very little interaction or gossiping between these adults. For the most part, I was with the horses and, although I ate my lunch with the other kids, that was all I did because I was pretty shy and didn't mix well. Of course, a horse can't talk and tell anyone whatever I say to them, so Peter must have felt comfortable leaving me there. It was the perfect cover to mask all the evil.

Also, like Christine, it was great leverage to get me to do what he wanted me to do. Once, I refused to give a bloke a blow job in his car and Peter dragged me out of that car quicker than anyone could speak.

'You give him the blow job or I'll sell Humbug,' he snarled right in my face. 'If you don't do as I tell you, you won't go to the barn for the next week. Then what will Humbug do without you?'

Another favourite jibe was, 'Just how important is Humbug to you, Beverli? Do you know how many jars of

glue that Humbug would make?' God, it was torture and, as such, it created a huge worry for me because I knew that I couldn't upset or trust this man, not after the things he was making me do in private.

At other times he would threaten he was going to hurt Humbug and, only once, he really did. I had argued with him while he was waiting for me to finish my horse chores and feed Humbug. I remember he had a client waiting for me and I was taking far too long because I didn't want to go and he knew it.

'You are going to bloody well go with me and you are going to hurry up!' he snapped and he whacked Humbug around the head. He was so quick it took poor Humbug by surprise and he felt the full brunt of Peter's hand against his soft, beautiful face. 'Do you want me to carry on? Because I will hurt your horse, I promise you, Beverli.'

That was definitely enough to make me hurry up. 'No, Dad, please leave Humbug alone,' I begged through the hot salty tears that streamed down my face. 'Please don't do anything else to him. I'll be quick. I'll come with you. I will do anything you want me to do, just don't hurt him. Please!'

I could cope with Peter hurting and abusing me but not with him attacking Humbug. I would have died for that horse, and that one time that he hit him so hard, just to get back at me and to get my attention, was unforgiveable. It still makes me shudder to think of that time but it wasn't the first occasion that Peter hurt one of my animals – that was a long-running habit of his throughout my childhood, because he quickly learned that my animals were my life and that I would do anything for them.

So Humbug and the stables became my lifeline. Very often, I would stand in the stall with Humbug and he would rest his head on my shoulder or neck – he was so loving like that. Then when I was sure there was no one listening, I would open up to my one true friend about my deepest, darkest secrets. Humbug would stand there and listen as I quietly told him about the horrors of the night, or the week, before and he would let me cry into his face for as long as it took for me to pull myself together and regain my composure.

Sometimes I would get to the barn and he would be lying down in his stall in the thick, warm straw. I would open the door and creep and in to sit with him – often I would lie on his side and he would gently turn to look at me as if to say, 'It's OK, Beverli, you're quite safe now. I won't hurt you.' And I would stay there until I heard Joan or someone else call my name because, when I was with Humbug, I really did feel safe. It was if he knew that I was damaged goods and that I needed a friend and I swear he knew I was vulnerable because he never put a foot wrong when I rode him. He never shied at anything or tried to buck me off or to run away with me. I think he knew that I needed protecting in so many ways and he was that special horse that was there to look after me.

There were times when I was so upset that I needed to be on my own, so that no one would find me. I had a little hidey-hole in the barn between the big bales of straw. I had laid down an old horse rug to lie on and sometimes I ate my lunch there alone. Most of the time this was my absolute private place where I could sob and sob until I fell

asleep, worn out from all the crying and sadness. It was so important to me that nobody ever heard me crying or saw my tears, because I couldn't risk anybody asking me what the matter was and news of my upset getting back to Peter. That was a sure-fire way to lose my horse and wreck what little bit of happiness I had.

I think that Joan realised that there was a problem at home, although she never asked me, for whatever reasons. Maybe she didn't want to know the truth or maybe she wondered if there was something going on with Peter and it was too horrific an avenue to go down, so she never asked me about it. She knew I didn't like going home at night and that I was quiet for most of the time, especially if Peter was there doing his odd jobs. If only she had questioned it all and asked me what was going on. I wouldn't have liked it at the time and, yes, I would probably would have resisted and lied about everything being OK but, if someone had cared enough to drag the truth out of me, the abuse might have stopped.

There was a young boy called Phillip, a couple of years older than me, who rode at the barn, and he was allowed to exercise Joan's own horses, as well as those of the people who didn't have time to ride their animals on a regular basis. He was a brilliant rider and a very sweet guy. We became firm friends and we would ride together in the schooling arena or would go out for long hacks off-property to give the horses some variety in their schedules.

Phillip definitely saw that there was something going on and that I had a problem with Peter and he became quite protective of me. Sometimes Peter turned up early to pick

me up and I knew immediately why – early pickup meant that on the way back home we would stop off somewhere and I would be required to service one of his clients, or sometimes Peter himself.

On those days, my heart would drop and I would make whatever chores I had left go on for as long as I could. It was just me delaying the inevitable, but there were times when I managed to keep Peter waiting for so long that he would have to take me straight home to avoid arousing Christine's suspicion as to why we were late. Although if that happened Peter would wait until I finally got in the car and he would let rip, screaming obscenities at me and threatening me with everything he could possibly think of.

Sometimes Phillip would butt in and tell Peter, who usually got out of the car to come and find me, that I wasn't finished and I would be a while. Then he would watch Peter's every move while he was with me, to the point that it would really get Peter's back up and he would say horribly cruel things to Phillip and me.

'What's going on with you and Phillip?' he would demand. 'I know that you and he hide out in the hay barn sometimes.'

'Nothing!' was always my answer and that just seemed to make him even madder, as if he thought that I was lying to him.

'Is he touching you?' he would ask, and the look of rage in his eyes and the madness burning behind them would bore into me. He would grab my arm and drag me to the field toilet and, pulling my riding trousers down to my knees, he would shove soap or tobacco (from a ripped-up

cigarette or from his tobacco pouch) angrily up my arse as a punishment. The pain was terrible. Sometimes itchy, at other times a dull ache, but enough to make me fidget. Even when I had tried to soothe myself with cold water and gone to the loo, it remained sore. On the way out, as he passed Phillip, he would snarl like a junkyard dog: 'I hope you don't think that you're good enough for Beverli!' Or another favourite was: 'What makes you think that Beverli would like someone like you?'

I could tell that it hurt Phillip when Peter talked to him like that but he never stopped being my friend. In fact, I think he was going through some trauma of his own at home because he put on a lot of weight in a short amount of time. I never asked him what was going on and he never asked me either, but there was somehow this unwritten bond between us. I think we both knew that the other was going through some serious shit that we couldn't talk about for fear of reprisals. But just knowing that made us grow close.

With the benefit of hindsight and age, I know why Peter took such a dislike to Phillip. I was Peter's personal property to use and abuse whenever and wherever he so chose to do so. Phillip was a potential threat and, as such, he had to be taken out of the equation. Peter made Phillip know how much he disliked him and those horrible snide remarks were designed to make Phillip think twice about being my friend. Again, it was all about control, and Peter had to have absolute control over me for as much of the waking day as he possibly could. When he wasn't with me, the only way he could take that control was by

threatening to take away anything he didn't like – and, sadly, that was Phillip.

Thankfully, he didn't put Phillip off being my friend and I am so grateful to Phillip for standing by me and making those teenage days bearable. Phillip, along with my time at the stables, turned a horrible situation into something good, at least while I was there. Even though sometimes I broke down and cried, it was still OK because I had released those powerful emotions that I was bottling up before they did me any more harm.

Humbug though – well, he was my ultimate saviour during those darkest of days. On the happier times we spent together, we would play in the field, or I would sing softly to him while I groomed him. He adored toffees and he would pull this very funny, distorted face when he ate one, which had me in fits of childish giggles for ages after. I'd spend hours with him in his stall snapping his photograph with my instamatic camera and Humbug would pose for me like a little star.

Our relationship was honest, basic and fulfilling for both of us. I spoiled him rotten, giving him all the love and attention he could possibly want, and he, in return, became my best friend and confidante, someone I trusted with the most intimate details of my life and someone who brought such joy to my life, such as I had never really known before.

I was heartbroken when I was forced to sell him when I was 14 because Peter had decided that he was going to uproot the whole family and move to South Africa for a better way of life. Another old man bought him and he returned to his roots as a driving pony but I never forgot

him. In fact, I can still see him in my mind as clear as day, giving me a horsey hug or pulling that daft face when he took a toffee, and my heart still melts for him. Humbug made such a difference to a child whose innocence had long been taken away. He helped me to be a child again whenever I saw him and, for that, I will always love my first lad. My Hummy.

CHAPTER SEVEN

SOMETHING SOFT IN SOUTH AFRICA

When Peter told us that we were going to be moving away to South Africa, I didn't want to go. I don't even think I knew where South Africa was, or how far away it was, but I didn't want to leave the woman I thought to be my grandmother, Sarah. I lived for her visits once a week, when we could spend quality time together at the beach or at her house making fairy cakes and doing other girly things. Sarah was my best friend in the world and she loved me more than anyone, so to leave her was horrific.

Lord, have mercy on my soul.

Peter was no longer self-employed by this time, having taken a job with a local tiling company. As he had refused the national role in the UK that his company had offered him, they had offered him a promotion in South Africa, the tip of beyond the horizon. He would keep the title of National Sales Manager at the tiling company he worked

for, but in South Africa it would be a much bigger operation. This meant a lot more money and nice benefits, like an executive car, a large expense account, gold-level medical insurance, 30 days' annual vacation, and all his travel and food expenses were paid too. It was an incredible deal for those days and one that could possibly have set him and Christine up for the rest of their lives. I don't know whether Christine wanted to go or not – I never heard her say anything to the contrary, but she must have felt out of her depth like I did. South Africa would prove to be a hell of a lot different to Plympton.

I thought about the future: would Peter stop what he had been doing – the sexual abuse and pimping me out? Moving away, would I remain powerless and distraught for years, just in another country?

When I checked out the books at our library all about South Africa, I remember feeling even more afraid. The books said that the country was made up of a mix of people from all walks of life and that it was a very wealthy country. The weather seemed unusual to me. I could apparently expect intense heat in the summer months. In England we had a few hot days but not every day. The heat in South Africa was split by electric storms – oh my God, what exactly was an 'electric storm'? I went to the reference section of the library and looked it up and what greeted me on the page scared the living hell out of me. I started to get panicky and it made me feel sick, like car sickness when I was in the back seat. The sheer size of the place overawed me, taking up the whole tip of Africa – Great Britain could fit into the country a few times over.

My heart sank – instinctively I knew there would be more men, more places like Bodmin Moor or the backs of farms to take me, more people to 'service'.

I continued to read that in Johannesburg 'the people talk fast and drive at high speed'. I had been taken to Soho in London before and the people there were a bit like that. I didn't feel comfortable in Soho with the ever increasing skyline of huge structures rising across the capital city – the place always frightened me.

I went into emotional overload.

After Peter agreed to the transfer, the house in Plympton – my childhood home – was sold along with some furnishings that my parents didn't want to take with us. Packing up all our belongings didn't take very long at all – we weren't taking that much because Peter had promised Christine she could buy all new stuff. I am sure that was part of the deal to get her to agree to move overseas, because she loved to spend his money. Peter gave her money all the time and she would spend, spend, spend. Always the best: nice clothes and fine furnishings. I bet she was excited at the prospect of getting a new house to do up, as she had ours.

Our boxer dog, Whiskey, was acting up. She knew; she could sense my heartache and she rested her head on my shoulders. She was a big girl with a stunning white chest and paws. I could feel her warm breath on my neck, the same breath that had become a huge comfort to me over the previous years. The tears started to roll down my cheeks and they splashed onto her paws. Her ears pricked up and she slobbered a lick of sympathy. She was given to

family friends Don and Jean when we moved, and they loved her. It was, however, only supposed to be until arrangements could be made, if possible, to get her out to be with us.

Everything seemed so final and I felt so totally alone. I was alone in England too, but 6,000 miles away I would be utterly and totally on my own. I knew that I would have no one in South Africa to talk to, but I prayed every night that the abuse would stop now that Peter had such a good job that paid a lot more money. Maybe he wouldn't have to prostitute me out to all and sundry like a cheap piece of meat? In my youthful mind, I thought, who on earth did he know in South Africa anyway? Who could, or even would want to, facilitate his sexually abusive pornographic ways? Crikey, how naïve was I? Paedophiles and child-sex-abuse rings exist the world over – 'like attracts like'. They seem to gravitate towards each other and they stick together like shit to a blanket.

When we got to South Africa, Peter and Christine chose to build their own house on a small plot of land in Gauteng, one of the nine provinces of South Africa. Johannesburg was the capital of the province and it was an area of high economic growth, which is why the tiling company was based there. As Peter was a master builder, he had hired an architect and designed his own house to Christine's specifications. She, of course, had a huge say in the way everything was built so that it really was a palace fit for a queen. Just how much of that mansion was paid for by my pimping episodes I will never know.

The house was built in an L shape with sliding glass windows looking out onto a crazy-paved decking area, which led to a top-of-the-range Penguin swimming pool in the shape of the playing card the 'club of spades'. The surrounding pool area had raised black-brick borders lined with palm trees. At the far end near the decorative wall the garden was awash with colourful plants – agapanthus and red, orange and yellow cannah for height and colour. The gardeners were attending to the planting of the garden at the same time that the house was being built, as the land was so vast and the soil poor. A tractor had to plough tons of compost into the soil along with chicken fertiliser where the lawns would be laid just before we moved in.

Living there was potentially dangerous because of the civil war at the time and all the hostility between the white men and the native South Africans, so it was imperative that we were safe at all times. A seven-foot-high wall was built around the property with a secondary wall by the swimming pool, and gates with extra security on them were installed. We also had to have bars on the outer windows, which gave the place a prison-like feel to it. The roof was wired with electric cabling that was attached to a generator, which at night was switched on, so as to electrocute any-one trying to gain access to the house by lifting roof tiles. Christine was perpetually paranoid about people breaking in, so it never felt safe. I picked up on her constant anxiety and found myself always looking out through the windows, searching for possible intruders. I think all of us were a bit jumpy, especially in the first few weeks.

As is customary over there, we had a staff of two

gardeners, three stable hands and a head groom to look after the grounds. Inside, we had a cook, a housekeeper who headed up the rest of the household staff, and a junior house lady, whose role it was to learn to use a computer so that she could order groceries from the local shop. She was also responsible for doing the washing and the ironing. Christine had one personal servant and also a gardener, who she shared with the neighbour, half a week each, so she carried on as if she was Lady Muck. She loved having servants – I think that she felt she had gone up in the world – and she talked to them as if they were the lowest of the low, which I hated. She soon forgot where she came from, that's for sure.

In the upper regions of what was the Gauteng province, everything was sand or beige coloured. I didn't like the dry scratch grass and the sand, dirt and dust constantly blowing up. Water was scare and there was a drought for over five years. I missed the green parks of Plymouth, the fields and the trees of the British countryside, always so rich in their colours. In South Africa there were no pretty colours. It was such a barren landscape, with just the odd few houses dotted around with greenish lawns that were watered every day for hours on end to maintain their lushness.

I also missed being by the sea and I soon learned that the countryside in the areas closer to the coast was lovely and green, so I begged Peter to move us to the coast several times. Christine wasn't having any of it though, because her palace was finished and she wanted to enjoy it. She didn't seem to mind the monotonous landscape because

she rarely ventured out of our house and its grounds. There was never a reason to. It was considered too dangerous to pop to the local store for food and there weren't clothes shops like in the UK that she could browse around alone. It was a very different life for us all but, so long as she had her Tracy, she could cope. I doubt if it occurred to her that I didn't like it – she didn't give a damn about me.

I never settled in South Africa – I couldn't. I missed England so very much that sometimes I would be in tears if a programme about home came on the television, and for days after I would feel depressed and pray to God to let me go back to England and to Sarah. I missed being around horses tremendously, I longed to see green fields and trees, rolling hills and I wished that I could get out of our house, which was effectively a prison, and ride to my heart's content. Living over there was like being in prison – not being allowed to walk off property for fear of being mugged or killed made me feel trapped within the four walls of our home. Even there, though, I didn't feel a sense of peace because I lived in fear of someone breaking in and killing us all. I know it sounds far-fetched but that is exactly what it was like. Even though I suffered the horrible abuse in England, I always had my horse and the freedom to breathe in the English air without the very real fear that someone was going to set off a bomb or attack me – now it was all gone and I felt so unhappy and alone.

The only good thing about the move, for me, was that, when we arrived, no one knew me from Adam. No one was aware of my sordid past at the hands of Peter and his

cronies, so it was a huge bonus for me. England seemed so far away, with all the paedophilia parties and the ugly, middle-aged men with their groping hands and thick penises. It was a relief not to have to think about them and, as a result, my brain started to shelve the memories of the early abuse into a place in my mind where I couldn't find them. Maybe this process was to help me to start afresh in South Africa. The only bits and pieces that I recalled were the last few years of my teenage life from about 13 onwards, when Peter raped me and took my virginity, and the sexual abuse thereafter. It was bad enough to still haunt me in my sleep, but during the day I was able to keep the memories and the feelings at bay until they became distant, almost not real, like a nightmare. It was only when I heard about a rape case in the news, or I read about a court case in the local newspaper, that the memories did come crashing back in vivid Technicolor.

There were times when I felt desperate for forgiveness, because I blamed myself for the rapes, which is a reaction that is all too common in rape and sexual-assault victims. The only way I could be forgiven was to throw myself into religion. We joined the local Catholic Church, where I hoped I would find someone who could help to make sense of what had happened to me. I hoped that the church would, in some way, save me and take away all the shadows and darkness that clouded my life. One day I had managed to sneak out of the house, which was a hugely punishable offence, and I had walked to church.

I fell forward at the altar as the sun shone through the brightly coloured windows, making rainbows in the dust.

As I lay on my belly on the stone-cold floor, I immediately felt a sense of calm come over me, as if God knew what was happening and was with me. Slowly and with reverence and respect for my surroundings, I crept and crawled up to the huge crucifix, which stood magnificently on the wall at the back of the altar. I reached forward and brushed a quick but meaningful kiss on the bleeding nailed feet of Christ the Saviour, the symbol of Jesus on the cross.

I cried out to God in my pain and begged for change and for the intervention of Our Lady Mother of Mercy, Mother Mary. I pleaded for her to intercede on my behalf. I began to recite the prayer 'Hail Mary, full of Grace, the Lord is with thee,' and I continued sitting at the foot of the cross on the floor, rocking as I went, tears streaming down my face. Sobbing in silence, time felt like it stood still right then.

At that moment, a priest came out from a back room and he was curious to discover why I was in such a state. 'Sit with me, child,' he said kindly. 'Tell me what's troubling you and maybe God can help you.' I stared at his old, withered face and I couldn't stop sobbing. He was so nice. He put his arms around me and I cried into his robes.

'My dad raped me,' I said, and the Priest looked a little taken aback. I wondered if he had ever heard that from any of his parishioners.

'Child, I doubt that's what happened. You must have made a mistake.'

I knew there and then that he wasn't going to believe me. For whatever reason, this kindly man who was supposed to symbolise all that is good in this world was not going to

help me. I didn't want to say another word after that because I didn't want to be called a liar. I told him that I had to get home and I ran from the church as fast as I could, sobbing as I went.

Christine decided that I should meet more people my own age, so she said I should offer to help at the church's monthly discos for teenagers. I wasn't overly interested in meeting anyone, boy or girl. I had morphed into my own little world and I wasn't keen on letting anyone in. Psychologically, I'd already had my fill of men and what they stood for, which was sex and nothing else. I went along anyway to pacify Christine, who thought she'd done me a huge favour by letting me out of the house to meet people of my own age. It was probably another way of getting rid of me while she concentrated on her house and on Tracy.

I joined the church 'fellowship' and, to my surprise, I did find the young people I met to be supportive and friendly. I didn't breathe a word about the sexual abuse for fear that they would judge me and, anyway, they were nice to me, all of them. For the first time in my life, I had friends, and I quickly found out that the boys especially liked me, something I didn't facilitate. I was never the flirty type, tending to keep the boys at arm's length but their interest in me was so innocent, completely unlike the interest that Peter and his cronies showed me.

Once, a tubby lad decided he would try to kiss me and he sneaked one on me when we were standing outside one evening. He was quite brave and he kissed me on the cheek, close to my lips but, as I had absolutely no idea

what to do in the situation, I froze on the spot. Just as well he took it as me being innocent and not knowing what to do. I could have hit him and pushed him off but I didn't – I think because I didn't want to show my emotions and I certainly didn't want him to know that something deeply psychological and weird was going on. I was accepted by everyone who knew me and, if I'd have reacted differently to that kiss, I know that people would have looked at me in another way. Little did he know that I knew very well how to kiss a boy and I also knew how to do a lot more than that.

I continued to be part of the Catholic fellowship until we had an open-evening disco, which included the church across the way, a Presbyterian group of young people. Everyone in the group was friendly and well behaved, except one. This teenager called Steven was very forward with an aggressive attitude. He was a very pretty boy and he made it clear that he was very attracted to me and, in a way, I think he had an idea that I had gone far further than anyone he knew. Men seemed to always know that about me – it was if I had a sign across my forehead that said: 'I'm not a virgin – I'm available.' We struck up a friendship at first and we got on well – he didn't put any moves on me at all.

Then one evening, he came to my house to see me. He rattled the gate and I went out to meet him so that I could take him into the house to meet my parents. We were having home-made Cornish pasties for dinner that Christine had made and I wanted Steven to join us. I didn't like the pasties much because they always reminded me of

something sinister from back in England, and I thought that if Steven was there, it would be more bearable.

Steve was about 16, so a little older than me. He had a way about him and was very interested in what I liked to do and who I liked to hang out with. At first, I enjoyed the attention, until I decided that it was only because he wanted something sexual – wasn't that what every man had been about in my life so far? He wanted to 'own' me and be the 'chosen one', favoured and loved above all other blokes. In other words, he wanted to be the one to take my virginity and all that it meant. Well, he was a bit late for that and, when the realisation hit me that he only wanted me for sex, I got pissed off and I didn't allow him near me after that. I banned him from coming near me and he soon got tired of me walking in the opposite direction whenever I saw him coming. I bet he thought I was frigid or something – he wouldn't have had a clue why I didn't want him near me.

Sadly for me, my hopes that Peter's rapes would stop came to nothing. Not long after we had moved and settled in, the same old cycle of abuse started again, along with the same lies to Christine to cover it all up. It was clear that he already a network of child abusers in South Africa and he had probably set them up before we'd even left England. How naïve and stupid of me to have thought otherwise.

'We're visiting the hospital, Christine,' Peter would say. 'Mr "So and So" was taken into hospital and we're going to cheer him up!'

Christine never ever questioned why he was visiting people we barely knew and, more importantly, she never

once asked why I had to go with him. It was always a, 'See you later then.' She clearly didn't give a shit about me, but then I had known that for most of my young life. Peter, meanwhile, already had his paedo buddies.

He was able to meet with them at the Masonic lodges across the country. Being a Freemason provided the perfect disguise for his illegal, sick activities because no one would ever question him. He and Christine had a lovely life and they seemed to be the nicest couple. With his connections, they fitted in perfectly and soon she had made her own friends, most of them being Freemasons' wives. They were wealthy compared to their UK counterparts and even there they had everything that they had wanted. People in South Africa looked at us as the perfect little family, respectable and friendly, and Peter again earned his reputation as the kind-hearted husband and friend who would do anything for anyone. Christine enjoyed everyone saying what a great man he was and he enjoyed playing Mr Nice Guy, a charade he had perfected when we lived in the UK.

Once again, I was his possession; he owned me and he pimped me out wherever and whenever he could. Peter continued to feed me a lot of sweet foods, just like in the Plympton days, so that my personal smell was sickly sweet, especially in my most private parts. Some men had lovingly told me that, even under where my bra straps had touched my skin and between my tiny toes and underneath my feet, there was a sweetish chocolate-like smell and a distinctive sugary perfume. The sugars evaporated through my skin and, again, there were specific men that found me very stimulating. Those men paid Peter to take me to some-

where very warm where I would sweat and, therefore, my smell would become even stronger and fill the air, so they would get their cheap thrills. Often, they would buy my underwear, just as they had done back in the UK and, as ever, Peter would then replace my knickers with new ones.

Men in South Africa were just like Peter's clients in England. They loved anal sex, they wanted blow jobs as usual, and they lusted after full-blown vaginal sex. Some of them brought their own range of enhancements along with them for a more exciting session. There were some odd-looking things that I was asked to put up my backside and also to do the same to them. Several men liked to have beads thrust up there while I stimulated them; others liked touching me using dildos and their own chubby fingers. There were others who seemed to be confused as to their gender, because they would turn up dressed as women, but then wanted me to suck their penises. What a depraved, mixed-up bag of bastards I had to deal with.

I yearned for freedom, fairness and responsibility for my own actions, and not to be forced to take responsibility for the actions of others. In the future, somehow, I promised myself I wasn't going to be sold any more.

When I would get back to the safety of my room in the house, I'd clean up as usual and hide in my bed listening to music on my transistor radio or reading a comic, an annual or a horse book. Just like in Plympton, I loved my bed and my room – it was my sanctuary, where I was allowed to be alone. I remember lying on the long brown shaggy carpet while I tried to make sense of what was happening to me. Sometimes I could think about it logically and clearly,

other times I would cry hysterically and wonder, why me? Why was I tortured almost every day of my life? What on earth had I ever done to deserve my lot? There were no answers to those questions and there never would be during my whole life. So I would either cry myself to sleep or stay awake and watch the door for signs of Peter paying a visit. I would read, until sleep over took me, sometimes with the book falling over my face.

Peter had become greedy. He made a lot of money out of me – thousands – which was disgusting, because he didn't need to make any more money as his day job paid him so well. One Christmas, he bought Christine two, one-carat ice-white diamonds and had them set in a ring she had drawn for herself, so the 'Queen of the Castle' had the bling she had always wanted. When I saw it, I knew that they were real stones and I knew that they must have cost Peter a small fortune. For diamonds that size, applying the three Cs (referring to Clarity, Cut and Colour), the ring must have cost in the region of around £5,000, which by rough calculation would be in the region of £25,000 in today's money. Clarity referred to how many imperfections the stone had – the fewer, the more valuable. Cut, in layman's terms, referred to how sparkly the diamond was (caused by light reflecting from the cut faces of the stone), and as to Colour, the more colourless the diamond, the more valuable. Yet the cost in terms of my pain and suffering couldn't be calculated. I shook my head and remained quiet. I couldn't believe what he had done. There were no words for it.

One of the worst clients I had the misfortune to be pimped out to was Mr X, a close friend of a major UK singing sensation. Arrangements had been made for me to visit him by the said singing superstar, whose code name was 'Kitty'. I'd long learned that many of the famous movie and TV stars in the UK who took part in the paedophile parties had code names that they were known by in those circles. Peter was in touch with Mr X, whom I guess he had met through his contacts and web of paedophiles. This guy just so happened to live in South Africa but travelled back and forth to the London studios every three months.

I was collected before the allotted weekend with Mr X and I was taken to a cabaret club where he was working. He was a singer songwriter himself and he had asked Peter to take me to the cabaret to meet him so that he could assess what Peter had to offer him and to make sure I was up to his standards. He gave me a rose and a chocolate in the shape of a heart, a truffle that was given as part of the after-dinner mints, coffee and chocolates that evening. Peter had drummed it into my head that I had to be polite and a 'good girl' as always and, as Mr X had said that he really liked me, arrangements were made for me to go to his house for the night – a first, since Peter never allowed me to stay over at anyone's house. This must have been well worth it financially for Peter.

I was to see him again the next weekend – at least I think it was a weekend, as Peter wasn't working that day. By late afternoon Peter had dropped me of at Mr X's apartment, which was in a nice, affluent suburb. It was

rather small though, with a little kitchen, a bathroom, one big main bedroom and, on the other side of the apartment, another room like a study with books, which opened onto the lounge.

It was my first time spending the night away from home and I was pretty damn nervous. Peter didn't know this guy from Adam and anything could have happened. But I had to keep up the act that had been instilled in me so many times by Peter. Men always liked me to play the innocent little-girl-next-door type and this Mr X was no exception. He was pretty quick to get past first base and, as soon as I arrived, he led me into his bedroom. He French-kissed me passionately, then he wanted to have sex with me. I already knew, of course, that this was coming, so I tried to hurry him up. He had taken his clothes off and revealed a well-toned body, which was unusual for me to see. Most of the men who had raped me in the past were horrible balding men with beer bellies and rolls of fat on their thighs. This rape was certainly different. My mind wandered to horses, the lighter side of my life, and to thinking of other people in my life.

Mr X was certainly full of himself. 'How do you like my new music?' he asked. How the fuck would I know? I hadn't a clue who the hell he was and I didn't want to engage in small talk – I wanted the rape over quickly so maybe he might send me home a few hours early.

He pushed my head towards his erect penis and I disappeared under the sheets to blow it. As I moved towards his crotch area, in the light coming through the sheet I noticed that there were a few funny bumpy things

around the bottom of his penis shaft. I had never seen anything like that before. I gasped. 'What's that? What are those things there?' I didn't want to be near them, much less touch them with my lips.

He shook his head. 'They're nothing,' he said. 'They're just genital warts, you can't catch them!' I was still worried that he was a 'gift giver'. I'd heard from other girls in England about genital warts – the gift that keeps on giving – and I didn't want to be on the receiving end of such a 'present'. Certainly not on my mouth or anywhere else!

Through the night, we had sex a few times, full-on penetration – the full Monty as it were. While I was on top of him during one of the screwing sessions, the phone rang. He showed me a hand signal to be quiet until he knew who was on the other end of the line. He had been waiting for the call from his best friend 'Kitty'. Mr X became the seasoned actor (he was an actor in movies too), describing the acts and what I was doing in graphic detail. I was doing what we now term 'phone sex' and, by the sound of it, the person on the other end was imagining it and asking questions. He wanted to 'hear' Mr X 'coming' – to hear the pounding of flesh on flesh and the explosive spurt of semen. As usual, I faked screams of pleasure. I gave an award-winning performance.

After Mr X was finished, he went back to the handset and spoke to Kitty. They had a private joke, laughed and said their goodbyes. I asked where Kitty was and Mr X said that he was on a tour somewhere overseas. I was threatened and I was told that, if anyone found out anything, both Peter and I would be in big trouble.

I cleaned up in the bathroom and took out my nightdress, got into the only bed – his bed – and, eventually, I managed to get some sleep. I don't know when Mr X joined me in bed, as I never felt him get in next to me.

Mr X was up early the next day. The morning was difficult because he was in a rush to get ready and be out of the door. He made a call to Peter and asked him to come past earlier than arranged to collect me. 'She knows who Kitty is,' Mr X told Peter. 'You need to make sure that she doesn't tell anyone about me or him. Take care of it.' With that out of the way, he told me that Peter was on his way to collect me and that he was going to rehearsals and a fitting of some sort. Then that was it: he disappeared and I didn't see him again for many years.

Peter knocked at the door and a servant opened up for him and showed him in. He collected my bag and we left. I was quiet on the way back to our house. I couldn't think of anything to say. I hated Peter even more than before because he had put me in what I had perceived to be grave danger. Mr X could have done anything to me and Peter hadn't been there to defend me. I was so used to him being present when I was abused – well, being on the other side of the door having a fag while I was raped – and I didn't like him being so far away. Despite everything, he kept me safe from these people and, for the first time ever, he hadn't been there.

'Boy, you mustn't say anything about Kitty being on the phone in case someone who shouldn't know goes to the police, or worse, the papers!' Peter said. He called me Boy

when he wanted to make an impact. We were still in the car so there was no escape and I had to sit listening to him going on like a rabid dog with a bone. Nag, nag, nag, rabbit, rabbit, rabbit, on and on he went.

When we got back to the house, Christine was waiting for us and, for the first time in my life, she started to ask questions about where I had been the night before. I guess that Peter had concocted a story that it was a Freemasons get-together and that some of the kids were having a sleepover so that their fathers could have a drink.

She asked where I had slept at the 'Masons' overnight stay; where was the bed? Peter told her that I had slept in a put-you-up bed in the study, behind the door that led from the main hall into that room, but Christine wasn't buying the story. For the first time ever, she smelled a rat: something wasn't ringing true.

For whatever reason, something told her that Peter and I were telling lies and that I had been pimped out by her own husband. I don't know whether she'd had her suspicions for some time because she'd never let on if she had. She'd never asked me questions to get clues if that's what she thought. Suddenly, she flew into a rage and, in her anger, she picked up a broom, removed the brush end and lunged forward at me, shouting and screaming abuse, calling me every name she could think of, duplicating a few as she ran out of breath. She chased me to my bedroom, whacking me as she went. I ran towards the windows, looking for a way to escape into the front garden, but they were closed and locked, so it would have taken too long to unscrew the bolts. As I turned around, she was ready to

pounce on me and to hurt me. She began hitting me all over my body with that broomstick but I fought back. It was beyond my comprehension as to why she would set on me like that. I was the victim, for Christ's sake. I was the one who had been abused for so many years by her fucking bastard husband.

I managed to get the broomstick away and then, in my own blind anger, I smashed it in half against the side of the window ledge. I whipped around after breaking the broom handle and stared her square in the face, a newfound sense of courage within me. Screaming in a deep growling voice, I yelled straight in Christine's face: 'If you ever do that again, I promise you I will fuck you up. You'll regret it!'

She stepped back a bit. Shocked, she turned on her heels and went through the door. 'Fucking bitch,' I said under my breath, shaking. My chest was burning. I spoke to myself, looking at the ceiling, 'Crap! Now there's going to be shit!' I knew it.

I can only think that, following the years of abuse, the thought that my own mother blamed me for what had happened pushed me right over the edge. I hated her more than I had ever hated anyone in my whole life. She was my 'mother' and she should have known instinctively what was going on. She should have stopped it when I was a little girl, instead of turning a blind eye to everything that concerned me. If she was blaming me, I was most certainly putting the blame on her because, in my mind, she was as evil as Peter.

After Christine had turned on her heels and flounced out

of the room, she continued to focus her rage on Peter. They went into the front room and had a screaming match in front of the fire. I closed my cream-flecked plastic crappy sliding Marley room-dividing door and locked it with the small key, which I left in the door. Peter banged on the outside of the plastic barrier. 'Come and talk to her, please,' he begged me and he sounded panic-stricken at the thought that she knew his worst, most depraved secret. I wouldn't budge; I would not go out of that room.

'Just piss off, fucking go away!' I screamed at him. 'I'm not fucking opening up or talking to either of you!'

He tried to force the door open. I never knew that the plastic sliding door could withstand so much physical abuse. Impressive. I sat there, frozen but shaking, as I hugged my legs and tried to block out the shouting and chaos happening outside my room.

I knew that I was in such major trouble. I remembered when Peter would threaten me with cruel acts towards my animals and especially to my cats. I was terrified that he would hurt them to get back at me and I wasn't wrong. He took my kitten, which I had just been given by a friend, and he threw it with such force against the back garden wall that it died instantly, its delicate little skull crushed.

Something deep inside me snapped that night – Christine had pushed me further than anyone ever had. How dare she beat me up for the atrocities that Peter had committed? It should have been him that she took her temper out on – not me! Thankfully, I didn't have to stay under the same roof for much longer. I left the house that day and walked to the main road and started to hitch for a lift. A good

friend of mine, Farrell, who was much older than me, saw me from the other side of the road. I knew him through older friends and he did a brisk U-turn and picked me up. I was in my jeans and my T-shirt and I was shaking badly. Bless him, he was really concerned but I wouldn't tell him what was wrong – I was too angry and ashamed. He took me back to the house, where I sneaked in, got a bag of clothes together, took all the cash I had saved out of the hiding place in my dressing-table drawer, then he gave me a ride to the railway station, me in silence all the way. Farrell was talking – I could see his lips moving under his black moustache but I didn't hear the words. We pulled up at the drop-off zone, I whispered a quick 'cheers, thanks', got out of the car and ran for all I was worth to the station ticket office.

I looked out of the window of the train, unconscious of my surrounding. The guard said, 'Tickets, please.' I showed him mine and he clipped it and passed it back.

Farrell had called ahead and managed to find a cheap hotel in Hillbrow. He knew the owners as he had used them for accommodation when he'd had a gig in the surrounding area. They would be expecting me and wouldn't ask questions as to why such a young girl was checking in.

In time, I found a room to rent in a small flat and I moved to the city of Johannesburg. My landlady was an elderly Jewish woman – a widow – and she was so kind to me. I had a lovely single room at the back of the apartment on

the quiet side. I was pleased I didn't have the front bedroom, as the building was on a main road. My rental included breakfast and a meal each night, as well as council tax, water, electric and heating. It didn't include the telephone, so I had to be careful and use it sparingly. I had a few interviews and got a job as a receptionist/secretary at a glossy magazine. At the weekends, I was working as a hostess at a nightclub, serving drinks in the 'private salon' downstairs in the club's basement. The venue was a private underground, black-market gambling joint where people played the card game 'punto banco', complete with its dealing 'shoe' and illegal poker tables. The croupiers worked shifts and stayed for six weeks at a time. They weren't allowed any underwear in case they hid money in it. The pit bosses governing the tables were all men, sitting on high stools above everyone. I had heard that behind the lights in the ceiling there were people watching us and everything that went on – how true that was I don't know; I never saw anything. During our breaks, I would ask the dealers to show me how to deal poker, the rules, the unspoken decisions when the house would take cards or not and some of the other card games, such as 21, also known as blackjack. The tips were great – the more drunk the guys were, or the higher their winnings, the more generous they became and I made a lot more money. If they were winning, the house gave them bottles of champagne, cigars and cigarettes and platters of finger food, as a gift to congratulate them. The punters would get skunk drunk and promptly lose all their money again.

We were allowed to cash in the drinks that the punters

bought and, as I am teetotal, I had a lot of drinks to cash in. I was paid in cash at the end of my shift and offered extra shifts when it was expected to be a busy night. I would also swap shifts with the girls who needed time off or had dates. So generally, between my day job and the weekend work, I managed quite well. I bought clothes and carefully managed my money. I even had enough to start taking driving lessons and take a few trips to the coast.

I was finally free. I had control over my life.

I lost contact with Farrell – although he was my best friend, I didn't want him or his family to think badly of me; he had done so much to help me. I had met his parents and had eaten kosher chicken soup at Jewish religious events. He treated me with love, kindness and the utmost respect; I just couldn't share with him the secrets of my life. He was an upstanding member of the Jewish community. I was a Catholic girl. I decided I would leave him to remember me as just that – a good little Catholic girl, sweet, never been kissed! Farrell did check on my safety and wellbeing while I was at the hotel but, after I moved into the apartment, somehow we didn't stay in touch. I never once called Peter and Christine. As far as I was concerned, they were dead to me – they were all dead in my eyes. I wanted nothing to do with them.

I lived all over South Africa until 1999. I travelled back and forth many times to the UK but I stayed in South Africa for my children's sake. Eventually, however, when my children were older, I went back to England for good, arriving in February 1999. I sighed with relief to finally be

home, crying tears of joy as I walked down the steps of the plane at Manchester Airport. I had a job waiting for me and accommodation, organised by the company I had joined the previous year. Sorted.

During my time in South Africa I met and married my first husband. We had three beautiful kids but eventually we divorced and I married another South African. That marriage produced another child – a daughter – but that union ended too. I should never have got married – both times were an escape from my own little world; an attempt to conform to how society said you should live your life. Most women got married and had kids – it was expected of you in those days, so that's what I did. I thought I could handle it both times but, with all the abuse that I had suffered at the hands of men, it wasn't a surprise that my marriages failed spectacularly.

It wasn't until I was 30 and I had split up with my second husband that I finally gave into my feelings and acknowledged to myself that I was gay. Only then did I start to live as the real me, not someone I thought I should have been.

After the break-up of that marriage, I spoke with Peter again. He was with wife number two or three by then. She had two small girls. God, I knew what was going on there. I know I should have done something about it, like speak to his wife, but I was still terribly afraid of Peter and what he might do to me. It was a fear born of years of abuse and it never really went away. He was drinking whisky and beer by the gallon – an alcoholic. In time, I heard that he

was ill and in a hospital for the mentally ill, where he was also suffering from cancer. I don't know why but I had to see him before he died. Looking back, I think it was to show him that my life had moved on and that he hadn't succeeded in destroying me – my spirit remained and I was my own person. I did forgive him because it was the only way that I could try to forge a life for myself. Granted, I had to reach deep within myself but it was necessary for me to do this to achieve any sort of peace. He could see that no one owned me, not even him, and I wanted him to see me as a happier woman, not the scared little girl who had grown up in his care.

Christine and I also forged a relationship of sorts years later. She had found out about Peter's sordid past. We never ever spoke about it – our relationship, such as it was, was on my terms. I chose to make my peace with her because she was the person who had brought me up trying to be a mother – or so I'd thought – and I considered, in her case, that blood is thicker than water. I afforded her my forgiveness in the hope that we could at least be friends – I wanted my mother back, despite what she had done. In the end, even that backfired on me when she told me I wasn't really her daughter after all, and that Sarah was my maternal mother. As I mentioned earlier, Christine was dying herself when she told me. I felt that hatred within me again, like on the day of the fight. I could have killed her but I knew that she would die soon anyway. Thankfully, something higher than myself helped me to realise that life goes on, as my own life had to. I realised that I had just as much right as anyone to have a happy life, so that's what I

went out and tried to find: the one person who has been there for me every step of the way. Throughout the terrorist bombing and beyond, this has been my partner Tina.

CHAPTER EIGHT

TRULY, MADLY, DEEPLY

Yes, I am gay and I have been openly lesbian since I was 30 years old but, honestly, I think I have always been gay. I'm not sure if being gay is as a direct psychological effect of the endless hours of abuse I suffered at the hands of Peter and all the men who paid him to enjoy the innocence I had to offer, or if it was because I had unhappy marriages later in life, or all of the above. Men were always at the centre of the deep hurt and abuse that I suffered. So, for me, being gay was a deep-down feeling. It was, and still is, the inner calm of knowing that being gay is just where I belong. But who knows, I could be wrong in my understanding of my feelings, although I don't think I am because living as a lesbian is what works for me.

I've spoken to different therapists about my post-traumatic stress disorder (PTSD), which some experts believe has been in my psyche since I was a child and just

something I never knew I had, and the subject of my being gay always comes up. Several therapists wanted to define the 'gayness' as a by-product of my issues with Peter, and believed that's why I 'turned'. Those same therapists suggested that I should have tried harder at being heterosexual, so that those hundred-plus distressing sexual encounters didn't cloud my true feelings for the rest of my life.

But to me, that is a stupid way to look at it. I KNOW I don't like men in a sexual format in any way, shape or form. I don't like men's penises, or their balls, or their smell. I don't like a man's big rough hands, or the way they sweat during intercourse. I don't like the way it feels – coarse and hairy – when they touch my body. And I don't like the mental attitude of men when they have sex with a woman, particularly a young woman who shouldn't be engaged in sexual activity because of her age.

I knew from a young age that I needed emotions: love, feeling, sensuality, pretty voluptuous womanly curves, soft skin, long eyelashes, beautiful soft hands with manicured nails, frilly-lace underwear, fragrant smells and perfume. I needed everything that a man cannot deliver. In short, I wanted a person in my life who was definitely not male or in any way at all like everything I associated with the male species.

I went to an all-girls school and a teacher of mine had joined Peter's group of dirty old – and young – men who looked at me as their plaything to do with whatever they had the money to pay for.

One particular day – I was about 13 – I was told to go

to a locked room to collect a pile of examination papers that had been locked away for security purposes, so that none of us kids could find them. The teacher was very particular about what he wanted me to do. 'You need to find all the examination papers from last year and this year,' he told me. I was really rather mystified because I had no clue why he would want both of those papers. Suffice to say, it was going to be a long job, which would keep me in that room for several hours, alone.

As I was reading through the papers, desperately trying to find the correct paperwork I needed, the door swung open. 'Beverli,' my teacher said as he stood in the doorway, blocking my exit. 'What on earth is taking you so long?' I couldn't help but notice that he had a rather large bulge in his trousers and my heart sank, just as it always did when I knew that someone wanted my body. I already knew deep down where this was going and I was trapped, not only by the confines of the small room, but by the fact that this once-trusted teacher was keeping me a prisoner.

He pushed past me to the shelf and then he moved me towards a part of the wall that was free from shelves and paperwork. 'You need to be quiet,' he said as he put his hand up my gym slip. I had long ago learned not to move when I was told to be still – I didn't want to risk getting him angry and being beaten. So I stood there at his mercy and kept my mouth shut, my heart pounding so hard that I thought it was going to come right out of my chest. I was also fighting the urge to throw up, which wasn't easy, but I knew that, if I ruined this monster's big moment, I would most definitely pay for it down the line, either

from him or Peter, who would be most angry that I had let him down.

My maths teacher was so excited that his breathing sounded like an express train charging towards its destination. His destination was my crotch area and he arrived there quickly and firmly, with the precision of a heat-seeking missile. His bony fingers found my soft spot hiding within the high-waist, school-regulation panties that we all wore back then, and the pervert was clearly thrilled when he felt inside me.

'Beverli, you are so well oiled,' he gasped as he moved his fingers against my clitoris. 'Mmmm, other men have been here before, haven't they? But I'm here now.'

He unzipped his trousers quickly because he clearly couldn't wait to rape me. He removed his erect penis, then he wet his fingers and moistened my female parts, his penis sniffing out somewhere to bury itself for a short time. He pushed his penis into my body with such force that it took my breath away and I was lifted off the floor for a couple of seconds. As I stood there, defenceless, I started to count the shelves – one, two, three, four – in a futile attempt to take my mind off what was going on. I wanted to scream out with the pain. It always hurt – this was not any different – but I had learned to stifle my own emotions to protect myself more than anything else. I'd also seen, in the early years, that men liked it if you screamed out while they were having sex with you, so I tried to remain as quiet as I possibly could. There was no way I was going to give them any more pleasure than they were already getting.

It didn't take him long to reach orgasm. After he had

Above: Sarah and George Stoneman, my real mother and father, but also my 'grandparents'.

Right: My sister Christine. She and her husband adopted me, believing they couldn't have children themselves.

Far right: Peter Rhodes, my sister's husband, and my long-term abuser.

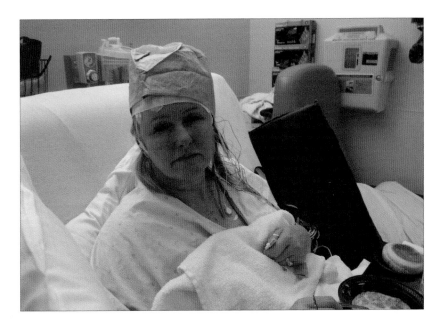

Above: Undergoing treatment in Bangkok, Thailand, 2007 through to 2010, for the injuries I received in the terrorist bombings of the Tube on 7 July 2005.

Below: My first lesson on Chips Tommy Girl. My specialist instructor was Lewis 'Blackie' Blackburn, who was visiting from the USA; the lesson was televised by the BBC.

Top left: With Tommy Girl in her stable in 2008, when we collected her from Dover after she had been flown to Luxembourg from the USA.

Top right: PP Chips Tommy Girl, American Paint Black Overo, to give her her full name.

Below left: Barely Whizable, or Whizzi for short, arrived in August 2007 from Canada.

Below right: With my partner, Tina, 'the one person who has been there for me, every step of the way'.

Me in Las Vegas, on the way to a riding lesson at Painted Dreams, after a journey that started in hate and ended in healing.

Inset: as a guest and fellow survivor, I released the white dove of peace during the 2011 bombings memorial ceremony in Canary Wharf.

raped me, he carefully placed his manhood into his pants, pulled up his zip and that was it. We carried on with the business of locating all those exam papers and no one was ever the wiser. It was actually one of the worst moments that I had endured thus far, because I had trusted this man, who had taken the trouble to help me with maths, a subject I found particularly difficult. I think that he had been helping me with my maths because he had other plans for me and he had wanted to gain my trust before he made his sexual moves on me. School was the one place where I thought I was guaranteed to be safe and I loved the six or so hours I spent there each day. I had been under the illusion that no one could touch me or hurt me; that I was free to be a kid again. Now this one teacher had shattered that illusion and I was completely devastated by what I saw as a massive betrayal.

I kept away from boys after that because, after the rape in school, I knew that no man could ever be trusted again. I also worried that they would find out the secret I kept hidden so desperately. I always thought that the boys had a good idea which of the girls 'gave it up' and which ones were 'easy' and those that weren't. I didn't want to be labelled 'easy' and have unwanted attention from those types of kids, so I prayed that they wouldn't get close to me to ever find out what was really going on in my life.

I think that's when I started to think about girls in a bit of a different light. A woman couldn't hurt me physically like a man could, and the girls I had as friends were good and loyal. I wished that I could be with them all the time. At the time, I didn't know what being gay meant, so I

didn't know what my deep attraction to women was about. I looked on it more as a trusting thing at the time – there was no way a girl was going to turn on me like all the men I had so far met in my life. Even my bloody teacher, whom I had liked and respected, had turned on me in the worst way possible, so really it was little wonder that I went to my girlfriends for the comfort I craved.

I found my inner feelings whilst craving the attention of my best friend at school. I wanted her love, in whatever form that was possible at that age. Initially, it was just her company and having time with her alone I wanted, even if we were just listening to records, or reading our favourite comics while eating ice cream. To me, it didn't matter what we were doing, just that we were together, alone. It was after the issues at school with the teacher, and the loss of my virginity in the way it took place when I was 13, that I found myself being drawn to her even more.

The summer holidays were a good excuse to spend endless hours together. We were able to go shopping and bake cakes in her mum's small kitchen – I remember that we even managed to make a few cupcakes and a heart-shaped pie. We had a love for all things chocolate, so we made Corn-Flakes clusters and added raisins, which turned out to be delicious. Our greatest culinary achievements were celebrated by sitting back-to-back in the garden, sampling all we had made and having a giggle. They were good times and for the most part they were innocent, as nothing remotely sexual had happened. We were just very close emotionally and I loved being not just around her, but being around her family, particularly her mum, who was so

lovely and kind to me. I wished with all my heart that my mum could have been like her, so, at every opportunity I had, I would go to my friend's house and hang out there.

My first kiss with a blonde, blue-eyed, beautiful girl would take place a couple of years later in the back of an old German Volkswagen Beetle. We were on our way to the cinema and we were sitting in the back seat holding hands, giggling furiously because we were so excited. As we shared a secret kiss, unfamiliar yet satisfying surges of electricity went through my body, starting in the pit of my stomach. I realised that it was pleasure that I was feeling as her lips gently locked with mine. It felt warm and it felt safe and I will never forget it, although that was our first and only kiss. I still look at photographs of that old Volkswagen Beetle and smile because it was the first time I had ever felt anything other than fear and dread when faced being in such close proximity with another human.

When I was a child, being gay wasn't talked about and it was definitely frowned upon with a passion. It was very much a closed, deep, dark secret, which was carefully hidden by men and women who kept their same-sex relationship literally 'in the closet', to quote a well-known phrase that is used today when people come out as being gay or lesbian to their family and friends. I think that's why I ended up getting married twice and having a family – not only was the first marriage to escape Peter and the abuse, but it was also to show the world that I was a happy, 'normal' housewife. Christine realised when I was a teenager that I was gay but she wouldn't talk about it, much less utter the word 'gay'.

When I announced that I was getting married, she said, 'Well, at least being married will stop you from living your life like that!' meaning as a gay woman. Back then, being gay was just not considered normal.

When I was 30, after two failed marriages, I started my first proper lesbian relationship. I was single and working in London, where I had a great job in the City as a business analyst, earning enough money for me not to have to worry about anything. I was in a great place financially and now all I needed was to find someone to share it all with – but definitely not a man! My first lesbian lover was the daughter of a friend who had been in a car accident. It wasn't a long affair but it was long enough for me to realise that, yes, I definitely was gay and that I wanted to live my life openly as a gay woman. I didn't want to hide any more, as I had done behind my two horrible marriages. It was really important that I lived as the person I knew I really was – it was the key to my future happiness.

By now, my sexuality was not a secret because, to be honest, I didn't care who knew. Peter had gone into a home for the mentally disabled, as he had a form of Alzheimer's and he was dying a slow, horrible death from throat cancer and emphysema, due to the many years of heavy smoking. He didn't care about me, much less remember who I was towards the end of his life, so I knew that he didn't care or have an opinion about whether I was gay or not. Christine was with her dear Tracy and she wasn't interested in me or what I did, so, again, there was no opposition there either in the end. My children didn't know about my sexuality at the time because they were

too young to understand but, when they grew older and found out, they were supportive towards me. They knew I had suffered in my marriages and they just wanted me to find something that would fulfil my life – they never judged me, which was, I think, rather amazing.

I enjoyed being in a couple of different relationships with women and I shared with them what I knew about my own life. Of course, at this point I had put all the years of sexual abuse to a dark corner in my brain, where the memories were supposed to stay forever. I told my girlfriends about my horrible, non-existent family life with Peter and Christine and my spoilt sister Tracy. They knew I had a horse and that horses were the centre of my existence and that they had been all of my life.

One of my girlfriends had been sexually abused by a paedophile when she was a little girl, a person who owned the corner sweet shop. As she was from a family that didn't have much money, and certainly no money for confectionery, she fell prey to the old man, who loved poor little kids, whom he knew he could bribe easily. He thought of himself as a generous character, who gave to those less fortunate. Instead, he was really a pervert who did unspeakable things to local children and kept their silence by giving them gifts of sweets and chocolates. My friend shared her experience with me and it sparked something within myself, a kind of inner knowledge and under-standing. I remember that I felt such an empathy and insight but I had no idea why, so I just had to support her as best I could.

Tina came into my life in 2000 and, at the time, I was

every bit the ambitious career woman. I was working for an American company called MCI, which is one of the world's leading companies in residential and business tele-communications. I had my little three-bedroom house in Milton Keynes, which I kept mostly for weekends because during the week I was out of the country.

As an analyst project manager, most weeks I would fly out to Brussels on a Monday morning, then I would work my way through Europe until Friday, when I would get the late flight back to London for the weekend. I was a specialist in my field, counter-terrorism, and generating new business, so it was a highly pressurised job to say the least. After passing hours in meetings, I would spend my evenings in my hotel room writing up reports, strategies and recommendations for the company's expansion and ways in which MCI could help with the threat of terrorism. Every three weeks or so I flew to Atlanta, Georgia, to spend a week with my American bosses, then I'd head back to the UK and start the cycle all over again.

It was a great job financially but I had zero social life. I had no one special and, when I lay in bed at nights, I missed that closeness with someone; a person with whom I could be relaxed and not feel constantly pressured into having sex with. I had no one really special and I craved to find someone that I could be myself with, and who would love me the same way in return, without relying on sex all the time.

I was a bit unusual, as I wasn't very sexually orientated and I hadn't ever had a huge sex drive. I knew that finding someone who would be happy to accept me as I was – and

still am – was going to be hard. Those who had been around me in the past had been very sexual and I found the pressure of sex emotionally traumatic on all sorts of levels. It brought me back to the events of my abusive childhood, especially when the person would throw a strop if I wasn't in the mood that day to let them use me, and very often their anger could last for weeks. Arguments would start as a result of my lack of interest in all things sexual, and I wasn't prepared to continue my life in the same way. I had to be with someone who shared my physical ways. I had to have someone to share my feelings and my life with and then, maybe, I thought, I might feel like a whole person. I had had a few failed relationships with women but nothing special and they had never worked for long, mainly because of my job.

The one thing in my life that I lived for, apart from my daughters, was my mare, Three Times My Lady, who I kept at a full-livery facility just outside Milton Keynes in Buckinghamshire. She was a Western horse from a very good blood line of blanket-spotted Appaloosas and was a striking steel-grey colour, with black spots on her flanks that caught the eye of everyone who saw her. Saturdays were our day together. I'd get up early and be at the stables for about 9am. It was funny because, whenever I drove into the car park and then walked to her stable, she would whinny so loudly, as if she was calling, 'Welcome home, Mum – I'm waiting for you!' I would spend hours brushing her silk mane and tail and her soft body, then we would have a riding lesson with my trainer or we would go off for a hack off-property down the beautiful country lanes.

My mare made all the hard work travelling the globe worth it. To spend my weekends with her were bliss – she was my total switch-off from the pressures of my job. She was my company, my friend and my confidante all wrapped up into one. I couldn't have lived without her and, like during so many other times in my life, I relied on my horse for the emotional support I was otherwise lacking. Indeed, that mare WAS my life at that time and she managed to fill the void that my job had created.

That year, however, I had heard about a new database that had been set up to help gay women meet someone. At the time, the only place that you could find advertisements from lesbians looking for love or companionship were in the classified sections of the *Guardian* newspaper and, even then, there weren't many of them. The new database was called Diva Dating and it had been set up solely for women. It was a bit like match.com and, after I had seen an advertisement, I was one of the first lesbian women to enrol and put my profile on there. I had to fill in all sorts of things, like my job, my core values, favourite films, music tastes and even state if I took recreational drugs, which I didn't. I set up my profile and, to be honest, I forgot about it soon afterwards because I didn't get any responses, and I then flew out of the country again for work.

Tina and her friend Patty had attended that year's London Olympia Gay Expo, a huge event for the gay community – one of the first in the UK. She was single at the time and she'd signed up for the Diva Dating database but, like me, she really didn't give it another thought after she had done it. I was sent her profile a few days later

because I guess we were a match and it was the first match I'd ever had, so I read her details on the computer screen.

I have to say I was very impressed – Tina's profile was amazing. She said that she was 40 years old and had a busy job as an audiologist for a Swiss firm of hearing-aid manufacturers, which meant that, like me, she was often out of the UK on business. I saw that, similar to me, Tina had been married once before and had a daughter who lived with her, along with their pet cat. Being a huge animal lover myself, the fact that she had a cat appealed to me possibly the most, because I thought she must be a decent girl to have a pet. Tina had posted a very nice, professional profile photograph too, and she looked very attractive dressed in a navy-blue silk top, white jeans and a little white biker's jacket. Her hair was done beautifully and someone had done her make-up too. I thought she looked a bit like a 'townie' – which I wasn't – but I was prepared to give her a chance.

Looking back now, it's something of a miracle that we got together at all. I like to call it fate. The phone number that Tina had put on her profile was her personal phone number and she hadn't used it for months because she normally used her company mobile phone. She kept her personal phone tucked away in a little drawer at her house. But when she broke the work phone, she had to use her own until her bosses in Switzerland got her a new one. And it just so happened that, during those few days, I texted her personal phone. If she hadn't broken her work phone, she might not have received my text for months and we wouldn't have met.

I sent her a text that said, 'Hello, my name is Beverli.'
Tina, whose ex was also called Beverley, immediately
thought it was her ex trying to get a hold of her and she
ignored it. I called and left her a message and said it was
Beverli again. At the time, I had a heavy South African
accent, so after hearing my voice Tina twigged that it
obviously wasn't her ex after all. Besides, we spelled our
names differently as well.

On the message, I said, 'Hi, this is Beverli Rhodes, I'd
like to have a chat when you're next available. I've also
sent you a text message. Give me a call to discuss. Thanks.'
I kept the message very brief and to the point: in a way, the
business side of me came out as I was leaving the message.
The last thing I wanted to do was to cause any trouble for
Tina if she was already in a relationship with someone. I
wasn't even sure deep down whether or not we would even
have the chance to meet up because both of us had busy
work schedules. It would definitely prove a challenge.

Tina called me back – she explained that, as I mentioned
earlier, when she first heard the message, she thought that
it was from her ex-girlfriend, Beverley, and that it was a
way of her stirring up trouble. We had a bit of a laugh at
that but Tina was very nervous, I still don't why. She was
babbling a lot and she told me all about the hours that she
had spent calling friends, trying to find out if they knew if
her ex had plotted some sort of a revenge call or not.
When she realised that it wasn't a revenge call and it
wasn't the same Beverley, she decided to find out who I
was and what I wanted. Unfortunately, because of our
crazy work schedules and the fact that we were out of the

country more than we were in it, it was months before we could meet up.

During our endless email and telephone discussions, we talked about meeting up in person many times. When I first started having contact with Tina, my previous partner was still living with me while she waited for builders to finish work on a small house that she had bought and was planning to move into alone. Despite the fact that we were no longer a couple we had an agreement that she would stay with me, and then move directly into her new home once it was ready. So as soon as I was totally free and my ex had moved into her new place, Tina and I decided that we would meet up.

In a way, I felt that I had always known Tina. She and I had become fast friends and could laugh, joke and talk about anything.

We chose Covent Garden in central London to meet up on a weekend in the summer of 2000. This is one of our favourite places, so it was a fitting part of London to have something to eat and catch a film or something afterwards. We both enjoy going to the cinema and we love bookstores too, so we planned to go to Foyles bookshop in London to browse through the latest books. It sounded like it was going to be a perfect first night together, given the fact that we seemed to have an awful lot of common interests.

I took the overground train into London and then the Tube to Covent Garden and, once I arrived, made my way out into the sunlight, a bit like a mole emerging from its hole. In the hustle and bustle of the lunchtime pedestrian traffic, I walked along the cobbled stones, cursing the

heeled shoes I had chosen to wear, as the heels annoyingly stuck between each stone. I walked towards the market at Covent Garden following the daily alfresco entertainment, which on that day was opera, and I started to feel a little bit nervous. I did have high hopes about my rendezvous with Tina because we were already good friends, and I prayed that she would be everything I wanted her to be.

I entered East Colonnade Market, which had a variety of stalls selling everything from hand-made soap to jewellery, handbags and amazing belts, confectionery and homeware, local photography and stunning artwork. I browsed as I walked. I had arrived early anyway to make sure I had time to view what was on sale, as I hadn't been to the market in a long time and I had always loved the stalls there with their ornate and unusual merchandise. I passed the pretty greetings cards and then I saw a stallholder I knew, Peter, and his ridiculously cute teddy bears. Looking at the bears, which were made so lovingly, made me smile broadly and set me in a good mood for the lunch meeting. Even though I was nervous, I had such a good feeling about our date and I could not wait to meet Tina.

A booming voice floated up from the indoor bistro as I walked down the stairs towards the restaurant, where the tables had been placed outside on the lower-level courtyard. I stopped on the landing area and looked down at the tables and saw a blonde figure dressed in white jeans and a casual jacket with a navy-blue top underneath. She had a glass of wine in front of her and she was texting on her mobile phone and looking around anxiously. Of course, that lovely figure was Tina. She was an absolute

stunner with her tan and beautifully fitting clothes. I held my breath and carefully worked my way down the stairs and through the summer crowds.

I approached the table and she waved me through when she saw me cutting across the courtyard. One of the first things I noticed about Tina was her bright-blue eyes, like a London topaz. They were instantly attractive and they drew me to her like a magnet. I saw that she was about a size 14-16 but she was definitely toned with it and I later learned that she had just got back from trekking in Alaska to raise money for charity. I liked what I saw – a voluptuous, healthy woman with curves in all the right places and a gorgeous smile to boot. Well, on first impressions, I felt that I had hit the jackpot!

After sharing pleasantries, we decided to go inside the main restaurant, as the noise was becoming quite distracting where we sat outside the bistro. A crowd had gathered and, between the cheers and applause for the musicians, and along with the clink of glasses and chairs moving, it was impossible to hear ourselves think. So we asked for a table inside where it was cooler and quieter so we could at least talk. Tina was so easy to make conversation with and I loved her infectious laugh – that's still one of the things I love most about Tina. We stayed for a few hours, chatting and laughing like we had known each other for a lot longer than we had. I knew that I wanted a lot more from Tina and she felt the same about me. It wasn't going to be easy to keep meeting up because of our hideous work schedules, but we were both prepared to make a good effort at making a relationship that would work.

I remember we had been together for around 18 months when we decided to take the plunge and move in together. I had been made redundant from MCI, which meant that I was in the country full time. Before that, I don't think I would ever have given Tina such a commitment for fear of the distance between us ruining our lifestyle. We decided to sell my house in Milton Keynes so that I could move in with Tina and her daughter in their little two-bedroom flat in London.

I spent a lot of time getting my house ready to be sold. I repainted it, I put little pots of flowers everywhere to improve its appeal as seen from the road, and I changed all the furnishings. My hard work paid off because my house sold quickly, which meant that Tina and I were able to move in together and start our new lives together. It didn't take me long to get a job and, before I knew it, Tina and I were in a fully-fledged long-term relationship and I had never been happier in my entire life.

There was just one blot in my life that I didn't understand. For years I had a recurring dream that terrified me to the core. It always took place when I was in bed and it was pitch black, so probably the time would be the early hours of the morning. In my dream – or should I say my nightmare – I would wake from an uneasy sleep to see a tall man standing in the doorway, leaning against the door frame and looking into my bedroom.

As I would sit up in my dream, I would see the figure smoking on a cigarette and the smoke would cling to his shape, making him appear as if he were in a deep haze. The horror I felt was sickening as I waited for the smoking

figure to move towards me, to come into the room and attack me or take me. As the figure would clomp into my bedroom, cigarette hanging out of the corner of his mouth, breathing heavily, I would try to move to get out. There was always a feeling of deep-rooted foreboding whenever this man visited me in my dreams and I would wake up screaming at the top of my voice, much to Tina's shock when we first got together.

Thank God Tina has a medical background because she was wonderful. She didn't judge me, she didn't tell me to be quiet – she was just genuinely caring and concerned that I was so frightened. Of course, now I know that the figure was very definitely Peter, and those deep-rooted memories that I had kept locked away for so long were visiting me at night, when my body was shutting down and sleeping. In my sleep, there was no escape from what happened. During the day, my brain could lock out the vivid memories to stop them from haunting me but during rest, bit by bit, the man responsible for the very darkest part of my life until that point would make his reappearance, as if he were mocking me and reminding me that, even though he was dead, he was never going to leave me because I was still his property, for ever and ever.

From those nightmares onwards, we had no idea what we were going to be dealing with in the early years of our relationship and it's a good job none of us has a crystal ball, especially not me. Just after we had marked our fifth anniversary together, I was severely injured in the London terrorist bombings and the deep-rooted post-traumatic stress and facial injuries that I suffered alone put every-

thing that Tina and I had to the test. Thank God we came through with flying colours and I will always credit her as my soulmate and my reason to carry on every day in the face of the extreme adversity I have had to deal with.

CHAPTER NINE

AFTERMATH

As I staggered out of the London Underground with the other survivors from the terrorist bomb that had wrecked our train and almost killed us all, I already knew that I was a different person from the woman who had got on to the Tube that morning. I just didn't realise how different I was going to be and, indeed, how my whole life and everything that I knew had already changed forever.

The attacks that morning on London's city centre will be etched into British history as one of the worst since World War II. They were certainly among the worst acts of terrorism on western soil in modern times and I think there was so much confusion because the average Joe-public Londoner just couldn't get their head around the fact that suicide bombers had pre-planned such a deadly assault with such deep hatred and loathing on the people of the United Kingdom. It was always in the back of my mind

because of the nature of the job I had once had, but, honestly, I thought that our country, Great Britain, the most watched country in the world as far as CCTV cameras are concerned, was a lot safer than it clearly was. I came home from South Africa for a better, safer life; a free life where I could sleep peacefully without bars on the windows and doors and without a weapon under my pillow, another stashed in the car and another .22 pistol strapped to my side.

At 8.50am that day, three bombs were detonated on London Underground trains within 50 seconds of each other. The first exploded on a train that had left King's Cross eight minutes earlier. The second device exploded in the second carriage of a six-car train that had just left Platform 4 at Edgware Road and was travelling westbound towards Paddington. This train had also left King's Cross about eight minutes earlier.

The next bomb went off in my carriage about a minute or so after we had left King's Cross station and it caused severe damage not only to the carriage where the bomb had been detonated, but also to the front of the one behind and to the tunnel. It was almost an hour after the attacks on the London Underground that a fourth bomb was detonated on the top deck of a number 30 double-decker bus that was travelling from Marble Arch to Hackney Wick.

This explosion, at 9.47am by Tavistock Square, right in front of my office, ripped off the entire roof and destroyed the rear portion of the bus. As the blast took place near the headquarters of the British Medical Association, doctors

and medical stuff created a triage in the lobby of my office building, where they were able to assist the walking wounded, of which there were many. Witnesses had reported seeing 'half a bus flying through the air' and two injured passengers said that they saw a man exploding inside the bus. It was just horrific.

All of the bombs were later found to have been home made using organic peroxide as part of the ingredients, and they were carried in rucksacks. I remember that, later on, when the police named the suicide bombers, everyone was shocked when Charles Clarke, then Home Secretary, announced that the perpetrators were 'cleanskins', which meant that they had been previously unknown to authorities until they carried out their attacks. And they all lived in the UK – they were all what you might call 'home grown'.

Mohammad Sidique Khan, 30 and of Pakistani descent, lived in Beeston, Leeds, with his wife and young child and he worked as a learning mentor at a primary school. He detonated his bomb just after leaving Edgware Road on the train travelling towards Paddington at 8.50am. That blast killed seven people including Khan himself.

The second bomber was called Shehzad Tanweer, aged 22, and he was also of Pakistani descent. This young man detonated the bomb aboard the train travelling between Liverpool Street and Aldgate. He also lived in Leeds, with his parents, and he worked in a fish-and-chip shop. Tanweer was killed in the explosion along with seven other people.

Germaine Lindsay, a 19-year-old man who was born in

Jamaica, detonated his device on my train. I've tried several times to remember if I saw him that day and I am sure that I did. The trouble was, like the other bombers, he just blended in with all the other commuters so no one knew what he had in his rucksack. Lindsay lived in Aylesbury, Buckinghamshire, with his pregnant wife and a young son. His blast killed 27 people, including Lindsay himself. What a waste.

The last bomber was Hasib Hussein, the youngest of the four, at just 18 years old. He was also of Pakistani descent and he detonated his bomb at 9.47am on the top level of the double-decker bus. Hussein also lived in Leeds, with his brother and sister-in-law, and, in that act of terrorism, 14 people, including Hussein, died. On the day of the attacks, all four had travelled to Luton, Bedfordshire by car and then to London by train. They were actually recorded on CCTV arriving at King's Cross station at 8.30am.

Much later, investigators in British intelligence discovered that the 7/7 plot dated back to the summer of 2003, when Khan visited a terrorist training camp in northern Pakistan. The camp had been set up by Al-Qaeda soon after British Prime Minister Tony Blair had sent British troops into Iraq. Shockingly, it came out that the sole purpose of the camp was to show would-be terrorists like Khan how to plan and carry out bomb attacks in Britain and even how to make home-made bombs that would cause catastrophic injury.

In total, 52 civilians died that day and more than 700 people were injured, many of them seriously. The London Underground and transport system was completely frozen

while authorities and police tried to work out what the hell was going on and it took some time because, at first, it was thought that there had been a major electrical problem on the train system. It was several hours before the police and emergency services recognised the bombings as acts of terrorism.

I didn't realise quite how badly injured I was until I got to the hospital, and just getting to a safe place where I could be treated was going to be a major challenge. All the signs on every motorway and side road into London showed 'LONDON CLOSED'. Tina, who had picked me up from the side of the road where the taxi driver had mercilessly dumped me, followed the road and the signs to the hospital nearest to us. She was very calm, which still amazes me when I think how horrific I must have looked right then, and she kept a watchful eye on me as she navigated the journey to get me to a safe place where my injuries could be treated. I was fighting the urge to vomit. The metallic, toxic taste in my mouth was getting worse by the second and my stomach, which was lined with my own blood, had been contracting violently. I was retching and I still don't know how I managed not to spill my entire guts out in that car. I just kept swallowing hard to stop the contents of my stomach from escaping. I figured if I could just hold on until I got to the hospital, I would be in a better position to deal with what was going to happen. I was in a great deal of pain but, again, I managed to push it to the back of my mind – I could not and would not cave in to my serious injuries until I was in hospital, where someone could help me.

Several of the main London hospitals that are equipped to deal with major emergencies were on standby to receive victims of the bombings. The nearest hospital to me was Chase Farm Hospital Accident and Emergency and this hospital was not on high alert to treat survivors, mainly because it's situated on the outskirts of the city centre and was deemed to be too far from the actual incidents to be able to treat the seriously injured. Of course, just like every other hospital in London and its outskirts, they had heard about the bombings and they were still prepared to treat people. As there were not enough ambulances to cope with the wounded that morning, many of the people who were not seriously injured were taken to other facilities by buses and I know that several bus-loads of the walking wounded were taken to Chase Farm.

I signed in at the area for admissions and I think it was only then that staff were becoming really aware of the enormity of what was going on. People began trickling into the waiting room and you only had to look at them to know that they were bombing victims. I remember that some people had a lot of blood on their dirty faces, others were crying, some quietly, others hauntingly loud. Some of them had arrived by bus, others had managed to get themselves to the hospital, probably by car or by hitching lifts a bit like I did. I sensed the feelings of terror that mushroomed over the waiting room like a fog. People were confused and begging for help, others just sat there, maybe waiting for their loved ones to turn up. I can't imagine what was happening at the main hospitals close to where the bombs went off – this truly was bad enough.

As I sat there waiting to be seen, I became quite sleepy. My broken body swayed gently as my eyes closed, then I'd tip too far and wake myself up. As I was not considered an emergency or at risk, I sat with the other patients who were deemed to be the same. I don't know how long I waited to be seen – it was a few hours, I know that much – but, given the enormity of the situation, I think that patients were dealt with as quickly as they could be.

The doctor who saw me was one wave short of a shipwreck. He was coming to the end of his shift and he had been dealing with the brunt of the wounded cases that kept on filing through the emergency-room doors. He was obviously tired and in a state of anguish himself. Unfortunately, there was a language barrier, as he was a locum who was filling in for another doctor who had got held up in the transport upheaval, which was showing no signs of stopping anytime soon. After the bombs had gone off, the London Underground had been completely closed and all other forms of public transport, including the buses, had also been suspended until the police and intelligence agencies got a good grip on what was happening. So that morning, not only were there hundreds of extra patients across the city, many with horrific injuries, there weren't the doctors and nurses to cope with them because many of them couldn't get into work.

In that situation though, I was thankful for small mercies and the language barrier didn't worry me. I just wanted to be seen and to be evaluated, and then I hoped that I could go home to my safe house. 'I'm not sure what kind of facial damage you have, miss,' the doctor said in

broken English as he gently pushed and prodded my face, particularly around the jawline and my cheekbones. I tried to sit quietly and not give in to the panic that was slowly taking a grip on me. I hadn't looked at my face on purpose because I knew that there was significant damage there and I was afraid to see it. I've always prided myself on looking after myself, doing my hair and make-up nicely and people had always said how attractive I was. The thought of seeing myself covered in blood with my features smashed in was too much to think about. It's not that I am vain either; I think that anyone in my position would have felt the same.

My doctor deemed that I needed a lot more tests and a full facial scan to find out exactly what damage had been done when I had hit the metal pole in the train. He was also very concerned about my being unconscious for 12 minutes, which he said could have caused brain damage. I was moved off to X-ray for the first set of tests but, as the day slowly wore on, I became more and more sleepy and shivery. I think that the shock of what was going on had come home to roost. I was given anti-sickness medication to stop me from throwing up and some pretty good pain-killers, so I was able to lie there while pictures were taken of my broken face, in what was the closest thing to comfort I had felt all day.

The X-rays were not showing as much detail as the doctors would have liked. They took a few more plates and a panoramic X-ray as they were looking at the detail of the hairline fractures in the jaw on the left side. The grainy images did not show the fine cracks in my teeth but rather

darkened marks and it showed that the bones in my jaw looked like a bit of cheese with holes, or perhaps a pumice stone. The entire overall picture was quite severe, showing that there was a need for immediate treatment for the infection that was fast building up in my mouth. I was told that the source of the pain itself was not the actual damage but the infection. The spongy tissue was becoming more infected minute by minute and the swelling was getting worse as time went on. In fact, the infection was already rampant in my face and jaw, teeth, mouth and down my neck. I was in a bad way.

A Doppler scan was done on my neck on the left side and it found a few tears and a build-up of blood in the main artery. This was causing an awfully painful throbbing pain that was hard to bear. I was taking way too many painkillers already and, even after I left the hospital and I was told to take a cocktail of drugs, including paracetamol and codeine coupled with ibuprofen, the pain never really went away, so antibiotics were prescribed. Looking back, I don't think that the doctors fully knew what they were dealing with so they just kept on trying different drugs and antibiotics to find me some comfort. The important thing, initially, was to get the infection under control, so a broad-spectrum antibiotic was prescribed.

I just wanted to get home, to get into my nice warm, familiar bed and have a lovely cup of hot sweet English breakfast tea. By the time I was released in the late afternoon, I was ready to go straight to sleep and that's exactly what I did when Tina got me home. Amazingly, I managed to sleep all the way through to the next morning,

which was a blessing. I don't even remember dreaming that night – it was as if I closed my eyes and my body forced me to stay asleep to begin the long healing process. I was so thankful for that extra-long sleep.

The following morning, a member of the Counter Terrorism Squad came to see me. They had called the night before and made an appointment with Tina to come the next morning while everything was fresh in my mind and I was able to give them a statement of what I had endured. The last thing I wanted to do was to go over everything in such detail the day after it had happened but I knew that I had to do just that – it was highly important for Counter Terrorism to get statements as soon as possible, not only to get any information that might lead to them finding out who had carried out these attacks but also to prevent anything else happening. The country was still on the highest alert and the prospect of another terrorist attack was considered extremely high.

I sat huddled in the corner of the sofa in our front room. The double doors that opened onto the patio were closed in case the neighbours were to accidentally overhear the interrogation session. The questioning itself was horrible, to put it mildly. The man interviewing me made me feel that I was in the wrong. I felt that I had to justify what I was saying with every breath. He wasn't a nice man at all. I almost felt like I was the terrorist – he didn't show me any sympathy, considering I had been involved in something so horrific and life-changing. All he cared about was getting the evidence down and finding out exactly what I knew and what I had seen. Without so much as an ounce of

feeling, he fired questions, questions and more questions. He would sometimes ask the same question but phrased in three different ways, as if to trip me up.

It didn't matter to him what had happened to me. I was not a soldier, not in a war, not fighting for Queen and country. Yet in war, there are no winners, only those that are left behind like us, like me – the survivors.

The interrogation was an ordeal, since I could barely talk because of my facial injuries and the misalignment of my mouth and jaw. My swallow reflex had been damaged and my throat was swollen, so I needed to push pretty hard to get tea and other soft liquids down my throat. Every time I talked it was like a red hot poker was being rammed through my face, causing my eyes to stream with tears. Unfortunately, the painkillers didn't do an awful lot for me. They kept the pain at arms' length but never really ever got rid of it enough to give me just a few minutes of peace to be able to relax.

The questions carried on into the evening. I remember that Tina knocked on the closed white doors, then again on the bi-fold doors that separated the living room from the dining area before entering the room. She forcefully drew the beige, heavily-lined curtains closed and she threw me a look – a flash of a stare. I could see she had decided that I'd had enough questioning for the day. She wore her 'don't mess with me face' as she turned to the detective and said, 'You need to leave Beverli alone.' I sighed, so relieved and so very exhausted. I was ever so grateful to her for taking charge because, frankly, I didn't have the strength in me to tell him myself. 'A whole day of questions is enough – can't

you see she was injured badly? You need to give her some peace for a bit,' said Tina firmly. The situation reminded me so much of when men had been abusing me for hours and I had reached the point where I was about to sleep on my feet and I didn't care anyway. Oh, yes, that bang on the head was bringing back horrific memories of my childhood abuse, so I was constantly being dealt a double whammy in my brain.

I was having issues with swallowing, as I had not eaten anything since the morning. Once I had arrived home to safety, I'd managed a few sips of tea, although it felt as if razor blades had taken up residence in my throat. I also managed a little bit of thin porridge that was easy to swallow. I just wanted to go back to bed, so the officer reluctantly agreed to leave and he arranged with Tina to come back the next day at 9am.

So I was completely mentally and physically exhausted and, while I knew that he had a job to do, I wished that he didn't have to come back again. I just wanted to be left alone, to be able to take it all in and process it for myself without the distractions of so many damn questions. For goodness sake, how many times did I have to tell him that *no*, I did not know the radical bastard who blew himself up and, *no*, I did *not* recognise anyone else who had been involved in the bombings.

Sleep became a great ally of mine in the early days after the bombings and I am so grateful for that because I was able to recuperate a little faster that I might have done without the rest. I know many other survivors who couldn't sleep at all for days after the bombings and some

who still can't, but I did manage to block it all out, for just a few days at least. It didn't take long, however, for the truth and the vivid memories to start haunting me.

The government, via the National Health Service (NHS), had sent out communications to all GPs across London, and the immediate areas that served as the commuter belt into London, that they should be aware that many of the victims who were treated in hospital would be having follow-up treatment with them, and that they should be prepared for an influx of patients. I was very lucky because I was the only 7/7 survivor to be treated at the doctor's surgery where I was listed, so I was treated by my own GP.

He was a very kind Chinese gentleman with a vast amount of knowledge, not just in general medicine but also in alternative therapies like Chinese medicine and acupuncture. I have always been very interested in using alternative therapies to help ailments, for instance colds, so I was most interested to hear what he had to say. He was very forward thinking and, by the time I saw him, he had researched possible ways to treat survivors of traumatic events such as I had experienced, so that he was ready for all the deep psychological wounds that could accompany the obvious physical ones.

I tried the acupuncture route for one session. I lay quietly while the needles were poked in my back. He twiddled about with one set in such a way that a huge pain travelled along a line down the side of my body and I started to bleed.

It wasn't nice, so I decided that this form of alternative treatment wasn't for me and I was pretty sure that I

wouldn't try acupuncture again. Sadly, as a result of the abuse, I couldn't allow massage of any kind because I cannot bear to be touched anywhere on my body in that manner, not by a man, at least. I find the whole idea of massages too personal and intrusive so, while it might have been a great way to help me relax in the early days, I couldn't face it. My GP even asked about reflexology but I had declined the offer – it brought back too many painful memories for me. I didn't elaborate on my reasons to the good doctor – I just politely declined.

In those early days, I just knew that this was going to be a long healing process, and not just to get physically better. And although I feared the surgery I knew I would one day have to endure to make my face look normal again, and to bring my jaw back into alignment so that I could eat again, it was the terrifying psychological damage that I was having to deal with that frightened me the most. I was trying to come to terms with being a victim in one of the worst terrorist attacks one in history on UK soil whilst also dealing with the suppressed memories from my childhood, which were the stuff of nightmares. I was in a very bad way and, quite honestly, I didn't know what on earth was going to become of me.

CHAPTER TEN

POST-TRAUMATIC STRESS AND MY RECOVERY

In the weeks after the bombings, I struggled with every aspect of my once blessed life. Eating was an absolute nightmare. I couldn't chew very well for the longest time and swallowing was a great ordeal. For someone who loves to eat and who values food as one of life's great pleasures, it was literally a bitter pill to attempt to swallow. Tina and I loved eating out and entertaining friends at our house but that all stopped dramatically and I thought we would never be able to do it again because, quite simply, I felt like my life was over.

My physical treatment started soon after the bombings and I was assigned to the London Day Surgery Centre, a very reputable facility where highly trained doctors specialise in a wide range of dental and surgical treatments. My specialist, Dr William Scott, had trained at the University of Dundee and had worked for several years in

a general dental practice. He had earned an MSc in restorative dentistry and completed a two-year M Clin Dent on orthodontics, and he was also well versed in all major endodontic treatments and surgical techniques. This particular branch of dentistry is concerned with the human dental pulp – the soft tissue between the tooth's outer enamel and the dentin – and periradicular tissues, including the prevention and treatment of diseases and injuries to the pulp and associated periradicular conditions. In short, he was most definitely the man for me!

William was, from the start, very accommodating. He had spoken with my GP and the hospital to understand just where the infection had managed to get a hold and through which pathway. I remember him telling me in great detail about what was going on in my mouth. 'Teeth are not totally solid objects,' he explained. 'They have a space at their centre containing blood vessels and nerves called the dental pulp. This pulp nourishes the tooth and the tooth can become badly infected due to deep trauma, just as in your case.'

He told me that, as the pulp is totally encased in hard tissue, it cannot heal itself and it seemed that the antibiotics I was given never cured the infections, they just kept them from multiplying at a faster rate. As time went on and the infection in my mouth became more resistant to the antibiotics, it spread faster and with some vigour to the bone itself. So the only thing to do in this extreme instance was to cleanse the infected pulp chamber and root canals and then place in there an inert, biocompatible filling. The packing and medication basically fills the space and pre-

vents the poisonous bacteria from re-entering the teeth to continue the infection.

During our first session, William had a good look around my mouth and took more X-rays and a further panoramic X-ray to get a better idea of the state of the tissues in my jawbone. To say it didn't look good is a vast understatement. It was an absolute mess. Holes had appeared in my jaw and it was looking very weak, almost crumbly. The infection had caused pockets of puss to form within the bone itself and there were obvious fragments detected by the X-rays that were very worrying. In fact, William had never seen anyone with the amount of damage that I had, so he made the wise choice to consult other specialists around the country and within the clinic to hear their opinions. I didn't care how many doctors looked at me so long as they saved my jaw and my face.

The overall decision was that William wanted to schedule a major procedure as soon as possible because, the faster he was able to enter the bone area and suction out the infection, the better. The sooner that the treatment could be introduced into the bone, the better the chance I stood of growing new bone tissue. I agreed to try out a new therapy whereby a special type of material would be packed into my jaw and left in place for six months to slowly coax the bone regrowth. The process would start with little islands of new bone, which would only be visible after six months of therapy. Holes would be drilled through the teeth from the upper area and these channels would be used to carefully remove the puss, infection and bacteria, so that the special material could be introduced

and left in place to create the new bone. The holes would finally be closed off with a temporary filler to allow the time for any gases and poisons to leak out where necessary at a later stage. Once this had happened, I would be ready to receive the permanent filler.

Another direct injury of the bombing was that I suffered mild brain damage due to the knock on my head and to the time I spent unconscious on the train floor. It was only slight brain damage but it was enough to affect me in my day-to-day struggle to gain some control over my life.

As well as balance issues, I was having problems processing language. I became desperately confused at times and unable to string together even just a few words to form a proper sentence. I was rarely able to find the right words to accurately describe my feelings or to give a description of what has happening around me. I recall looking at a bird eating from the bird table outside on our patio and I was trying to give a detailed account of the types of garden birds that Tina and I had grown to love seeing in our backyard. I could not remember the names of the little finches or even the type of bird table and seeds we had provided for our daily visitors. It was incredibly frustrating and, even though, as time went by, I improved, it was a slow process that impacted on my life greatly, especially when I tried to return to work.

Of course, my life and my work were spectacularly different after the bombing incident. There was no way they wouldn't be. The offices had taken a major financial blow at the time, as we were deemed to be part of the crime scene for the bus explosion, so all staff were told to work

from home and we were given a special computer sign-on for remote access, to ensure everyone's safety.

And I was able to log in and check emails and do as much as I could manage, which wasn't a great deal. I would sit in front of the computer, dribbling and not being able to swallow properly, which was painful and made it difficult to concentrate. Although in the first day or so after the bombings I had been able to sleep, the rest didn't last long. After that, sleep was impossible, mainly because of the severe pain I felt all day, every day, and also to the fact that the vivid images of almost every single second of the train attack haunted me whether I was awake or snatching a few minutes sleep.

I know that my work output diminished considerably as a result of the brain damage, along with my IQ. I knew it and so did my work colleagues. My line manager had little or no understanding of what I was going through. He focused only on his profit-and-loss sheet – nothing else mattered. I remember on one of my sick days, the landline downstairs rang and it was my manager on the phone. 'Coming back to work soon, are you?' he barked, less than a month after the event in August 2005. He was trying to make sense of my 'sick note', yet not grasping the difference between 'sick' and 'injured'. I didn't even have a chance to reply when he said, 'Instead of London, go to the Marlow offices. My PA will make a terminal and desk area available for you. There are no trains, no Underground and no police stations near the office.'

So I guess he had heard from colleagues that the sound of police and emergency-service sirens scared the hell out

of me. I also soon realised that he had heard that I couldn't face getting on a Tube train again, or even a bus or other forms of public transport, and I certainly couldn't have made it into the old London office at the time. I worked at the Marlow offices for the remainder of my contract. As the sympathetic Human Resources staff had to deal with many of the employees who had been caught up in the events of 7/7, they were well trained in being intensely supportive.

But the damage had been done and the PTSD affected me terribly. It made me feel like a prisoner in my own environment, especially when I was at home. I was afraid to go far on my own and, if I heard the wailing sirens of police cars, ambulances or fire engines, the sense of panic I felt was overwhelming and I'd feel like I was going to die. The sound of police helicopters also heightened my anxiety. I was also quite vigilant, always watching what was around me, taking note of people's clothing, looks, where they were heading, what car they drove, etc. – anything that would help to identify a person should I need to. I started keeping doors and windows locked at all times, with the blinds drawn down and curtains drawn. I didn't know at the time but this 'hyper-vigilance' was all part of PTSD. The house that was my home had also become a prison cell.

I'd always been very outgoing and independent, so to be afraid of going out, coupled with the intense anxiety that I felt whenever I was at home on my own, started to completely ruin what life I had left.

Sometimes the grief for my former life would overwhelm

me. I would often run to the depths of the back garden and hide near the shed by one of the big trees. My dog Beelie, a particularity small female Yorkshire Terrier, and a miniature Schnauzer called Daxx, who is actually Tina's little dog, became my lifelines. They would follow me down the garden with a ball or with their toys in their mouths, hoping for a few minutes of carefree play, just as they had grown used to having with me before the bombings. I would sit with the dogs at the bottom of the garden and cry and then I'd get angry, have a scream or two, beat at the shed with my fists, kick the tree, then psych myself up for the walk back to the house.

I was told by a therapist that my actions were classic post-traumatic-stress symptoms and that I was suffering badly. I noticed that I was slipping into the use of avoidance behaviours, so that I wouldn't have to see my loved ones or anyone else who might ask me questions I didn't want to have to deal with. Isolating oneself from loved ones is also a classic sign of PTSD. My whole world was rapidly collapsing because all around me all I could see in my mind was death. That is a terrifying place to be.

In the dark moments before dawn and during the nights when the nightmares were at their worst, a creeping sensation would come over me, as if I was being watched by a man in the corner of the room. It was the same man each time and the very same man who used to come into my room when I was a small defenceless girl – the tall man with rough hands, who smelled of Old Spice aftershave lotion and who had a funny tickly cough. I would lie in the bed after the dreams and feel the burn of sweat and fear

flow through my entire body. My legs would get goose-bumps – this was the warning sign that I was likely to suffer some form of panic attack. The memories of abuse, which I had first seen in the Tube tunnel of the train on 7 July 2005, were back with a vengeance. That creepy son of a bitch was back in my life. I was no longer really alone, just like when I was a little girl, and my every move was shadowed. The power Peter had once asserted over me was back in a big way.

My therapist has told me that I probably suffered PTSD after the years of childhood abuse I had endured, but that my mind had chosen to shelve those memories in a safe place so that I could get on with my life. It's not unusual in people who have suffered severe sexual abuse. But the problem can resurface if years later, as was the case with me, another prolonged trauma comes along. Most people don't suffer such a major trauma more than once in their lives but, in my case, that whack on the head and the bombing were enough to send my mind into overdrive and allow those most painful of times to resurface. It was like getting dealt two major whammies at once and that's when the PTSD is intensified. Ever since the London bombings, the PTSD has never gone away, so my life has had to become much more about learning to manage things effectively and using different coping strategies.

I was never really told what the actual definition of 'initial traumatic event' would be in my case, as it's all a bit chaotic, to say the least. My trauma started as early as the age of three, with the events continuing to happen throughout my childhood and teenage years. I had about

10 normal, seemingly stress-free years in my life after that. Then I hit 40 and bam!

A few months after the terrorist attack, I was treated at St Bartholomew's Hospital in London, where I had trauma therapy. The trouble was, the therapy was very confusing and, rather than help me, it caused me more grief. The junior doctor there, in an attempt to try to make sense of everything, started with the sexual abuse, referring to this as the 'initial' trauma I had experienced. He suggested that I had been suffering from PTSD for most of my life but hadn't known it until now. Some survivors were diagnosed as having 'complex' PTSD after the bombings but I was diagnosed as having 'severe' PTSD, probably because the two traumas surfaced at the same time, giving me two lots of memories and events to deal with.

I've been told that because of the length of time I have had my PTSD, it may mean that I have to learn to live with it. I think that's because it is so deep rooted in my soul and, as the years go by, I am going to have to develop greater coping strategies. Perhaps it's unlikely that I will ever fully return to the person I was before the 7/7 bombings opened my Pandora's Box. I try to look at every day as a bonus and, of course, some days are better than others – that's just the way it is. Although it's hard trying to live like that, for the most part, I give it my best shot. I know that I deserve to be happy after everything I have been through, and that's a really good start. Besides, my one constant throughout this ordeal has been my Tina.

Tina was my rock back then and she remains that way today. I still remember that day that she picked me up

from the road as I stumbled in the middle of the High Street on that July day in 2005. My personal blonde bombshell; my 'knightess' in white shining armour. Her sparkling blue eyes were filled with tears and her platinum-blonde hair glistened in the weak, patchy streams of English sunlight that morning. I realised it was her, even in my dazed state as she supported me, and I slipped into the front seat of her car.

'Oh my, thank Christ you're all right,' she said, tears rolling down her face, her pale English-rose complexion still so perfect, even in her emotional state. I wondered what she thought about my condition, dishevelled and bleeding heavily. She tried her best to remain calm the whole time, which I think was amazing considering the extent of my injuries, but I saw her shaking as we drove towards the hospital.

I know it took a great deal of strength and control on her part to stop the emotions seeping through and making a bad situation seem even worse. Since that day, she has been very modest with her own feelings about how she has been affected and I know that she has suffered a great deal too in different ways. She has been stalwart; a pillar, defending every action of mine against those that challenge my thinking. I know instinctively that she was close to losing hope of me ever getting better, but she never reached the point of totally giving up.

We never did the 'talking-for-hours' reaction to the trauma. Instead, we opted for just sitting quietly together in a space of total trust; a space where, if we wanted to share and talk through what was happening, we could. But

if I didn't want to, which was often, because of the PTSD, we gradually got to a point where we knew what each other was feeling just by looking at each other's facial expressions or body language. We both yearned for silence, peace and calm. In order to get these things back in our lives, we tried meditation to ease our minds and it worked well, as it provided a key to opening the soul where, for a few minutes at least, we were able to deal with all the memories from 2005 and, for me at least, even further back. Those times really did help me and I think, despite everything, where other survivors' marriages and relationships may have fallen apart due to their experiences of PTSD, Tina and I grew closer than ever.

And we both knew that life as it was before 7/7 was over. Apart from everything else we had to deal with, we were never going to have the same kind of money coming in as we'd had before – no more wonderful holidays abroad or the luxuries we were once able to enjoy because of our double income. I was never going to be able to hold down a management job again and I didn't have enough time to start moving back up the career ladder again. I would never again enjoy the perks of being a top executive. Although it may have seemed the least of our worries in the circumstances, my outlook felt bleak.

At the time of the bombings, Tina and I rented a beautiful house in north London, which we both loved, particularly because of the little garden at the back. However, to add insult to injury, a week or so before Christmas that year, we received a letter to inform us that the bank had foreclosed on the owner of the property, and

that we had to be out just after Christmas. It seemed an impossible thing to consider with everything that was going on at the time. I just could not believe our bad luck and I just kept thinking what on earth I had done to deserve so much crap in my life? What had I ever done that God felt I should be dealt such awful life cards?

Tina's mum and dad had come to stay and my daughters Sofia-Cyan and Shannyn-Lee had flown over from South Africa to be with us for our first Christmas after the terrible scare of 7/7. A week before we had been handed the eviction notice, Tina and I had picked the pair of them up from the airport and I was so excited at the thought of two of my daughters being with us. After the bombings, I had spoken to them at length on the phone but there was nothing like seeing them in person, being able to hold them close and tell them how much I loved and cared for them.

I found myself drifting off in the car, thinking about my girls and how much they had always loved Christmas and how, when they were children, I had always made such a big fuss over the festive season, so as to give them special family memories. Now they were all grown up with their own lives and they were coming over to England for me, to try to make my Christmas as special and meaningful as they could. In the light of what had happened, this was going to be one Christmas to remember and cherish because, if things had worked out differently, I might not have been around to celebrate. So despite my PTSD, I was determined that I wasn't going to wallow in what had happened, but to live for the moment and enjoy every minute.

We arrived at Gatwick Airport and the wait began. It had been several years since we'd seen each other and all that stood between us now was a thick glass door. So Tina and I waited and waited. It seemed like an age. Suddenly, I needed the loo – my nerves were on end and I rushed off to find the toilets. Knowing my luck, I thought, my daughters would appear out of the customs doors just as I reached the lavatories, but I had to go. I gestured to Tina that I was off to the loo and scurried away. True to form, as I rushed back to my spot at the arrivals barrier, Sofia-Cyan and Shannyn-Lee were there, waving at me. I laughed it off telling them: 'I had to go and pee desperately!' We hugged each other as if our lives depended on it, then we headed out of the airport building for the drive home. Picking my girls up was officially the start of our Christmas and the best thing that had happened to me in months.

Now faced with the prospect of homelessness, Tina and I contacted the solicitors and said that it would be impossible for us to move so close to Christmas. There were six of us in the house already and Tina's daughter, Asria, was also coming over with the security-officer boyfriend she had at the time, to spend part of Christmas with us. So Asria and him were going to have to use the blow-up bed. The house was full to the gunnels and there was no way that I was going to ruin that Christmas for any of us. Absolutely no way.

Thankfully, as it was nearly the festive holiday, the solicitors were understanding and gave us a delayed moving date of 8 January 2006. In fact we already knew that we would have to move out eventually, because letters

to the owners informing them that they were behind with their mortgage, had been sent to our address. So we had accordingly made plans to move to Norwich, where Tina had a job lined up. The trouble was, when we got the eviction notice we weren't at all prepared for the move.

So we had Christmas ahead to enjoy and make happy, positive memories that would have to last me for years to come. The plan was that, by the time the moving day arrived, my daughters would be back on the plane to South Africa and Tina's mum and dad would be back in west London. Tina's daughter would be back at work and living with her boyfriend in Littlehampton on the coast of England.

Christmas that year was, for me, a celebration, regardless of what I was going through emotionally. I intended it to be the best ever and I wasn't disappointed. Everyone was in a joyous mood, particularly my daughters and, for a short time, I was able to allow myself to enjoy what was happening around me. Part of my PTSD was 'survivor's guilt' and I had been suffering from that for a while. While this was something that my therapist said was completely normal, it was hard to keep under control. The deep-rooted feelings about why I'd survived the bombings when others hadn't, haunted me, particularly when I was lying awake at night or if I was on my own during the day. I had to tell myself that I was lucky enough to be able to enjoy Christmas with my family and that, for that short time, I had to make a special effort.

I managed to eat a bit of proper substantial food again. I had a plate of mashed potatoes, a piece of gravy-soaked

bread, mashed-up roast potatoes and cauliflower. Cold custard had become my best friend since the bombings, and I'd eaten so much of that I could have sunk a battleship with it! But on Christmas Day I had the treat of sloppy sherry trifle and, my goodness, trifle had never tasted so good! It was good for everyone to see that I was eating again and I think it added to a good Christmas for us all.

Our moving day arrived in January and, although it was colder than usual, it was bright and clear. We arranged for a removal firm to pack up the house. We had separated the boxes that were going to Cyan and Shannyn in South Africa, plus a suitcase of personal stuff that they couldn't take on the plane with them. I had wanted to have a big clear-out before we moved and, looking back, I think it was an attempt to try to let go of the past and look forward to new things. The movers detailed what was going to Johannesburg first and sent that on its way before they loaded the rest of our household belongings into their lorry.

When we finally moved to Norwich, I was happier than I had been for some time. It was a new start and I was thankful to be in a place where no one knew me as a terrorist-bomb victim. I could make new friends if I wished, or I could stay at home in my new world after my day job at Norwich Union – the choice was very much mine and I was grateful for the opportunity to start over, with Tina by my side.

Unfortunately, my newfound happiness was short-lived. In the months after the bombings, I was fighting for compensation from the government for the injuries I had

suffered on the train. My high-profile compensation solicitor was Jewish and he was a target of Islamic extremism. He had received threats to his safety and the safety of his young family too, which must have been terrifying for him. A threat had been placed in an envelope and stuck to the wall of the lift where he worked, next to a statement written in scruffy handwriting saying: 'Die you Jewish pig lawyer.'

The evil bastards had stuck a further envelope with another threat on a wall near his office in London. It was covered with fingerprints, and while I am not sure what the Met Police made of it all, they must have taken the threats seriously because my solicitor took some time off straight away to ensure the safety of his family. I didn't know it at the time, but not only was the solicitor being targeted, so was I, and the police thought it could be the same people: probably a small terrorist cell. I had been in the local newspaper talking about the terrorist attacks and my recovery, and I presume that the terrorist group had discovered that I was one of this solicitor's clients and targeted me too. I hadn't ever said anything particularly controversial during any interviews but they had seen me in the public limelight, they had my name and as such they could track me down and try to scare me.

To this day, I'm not sure how I was traced to Norwich but that's what had happened. I had, by this time, returned to work and, on coming home one day, my next-door neighbour, whom I had met only once before, popped her head in the front door and told me to go to her place quickly, as there was a telephone call for me on her house

phone. I grabbed my keys and followed her next door, wondering who on earth would be calling me on my neighbour's phone. Everyone who would have needed to contact me – my friends and family – had my mobile-phone number, so this was really weird.

I picked up the phone and was shocked to hear the threatening voice of the man on the end of the line say, 'We know where you live now!'

'Who is this, please?' I asked, but there was no reply. I knew that this mystery man was still on the end of the phone though, because I could hear him breathing.

Eventually, he said, 'We've got you! We know where you are!' And, with that, he hung up.

I was obviously taken aback. I thanked my neighbour, remarking how odd it was that the caller had taken the trouble to find and call her number but, so as not to alert her to any possible danger, I dismissed the call as 'run of the mill', and nothing serious.

With that, I left and headed back to my house. I was shaking with fear. I was on my own and all sorts of things were running through my head. Was the man part of the group who had planned the bombings? Was he a terrorist who wanted to kill me because I had survived? I tried to stop myself getting hysterical, which wasn't easy. Once I got inside the house, I locked the doors and checked all the windows and doors to make sure that no one could get in. I called the Counter Terrorism Squad straight away and, while I tried to remain calm, I was aware that I was talking like a crazy woman, and when my words came out properly they were spoken too fast to be intelligible. I

related to the officer on the end of the phone what had happened. I also mentioned that I was worried about the safety of my Tina.

All sorts of traumatic thoughts were swirling around in my head – for instance, what if they were planning to do something to Tina in order to get to me? The officer agreed to send someone round as soon as possible and gave the call a high-priority rating so that it would be dealt with quickly.

The officer who was assigned to me arrived quickly, within 15 minutes, and, as soon as he came through the door, he took a detailed statement from me, so I knew that he was taking the threat very seriously. He said that it could be a part of the extremist group that was trying to frighten the survivors, although why they would do that is beyond me. They had nothing to gain by issuing threats, although I suppose it would have been a very different story if they had chosen to act on those threats.

When I was on my own in the house again, I was on high alert. I was frightened. I kept the light off and moved silently around the house, checking the surrounds of the property at intervals and watching for unusual cars or motorbikes – for anything out of the ordinary. I remember that there was a black or dark-coloured vehicle parked up on the other side of the road for some time that evening, so I made a note of the car's number plate and called the information through to the assigned officer. He arranged for a unit to do a drive-past at intervals to check that all was well, which gave me some sense of security, although not a lot.

Tina was freaking out, to say the least. She was not used to threats of this type, any more than I was. She had also suffered trauma in her past, over 20 years before, when her ex-husband had attacked her and left her for dead. She couldn't recall exactly how she managed to escape, just that she had. Her defensive techniques had saved her up to a point, but she was still battered and broken, bruised and torn up. She had stayed in hospital for a time, during which period the police arrested him. Suddenly, once more, a very real threat to our safety had entered our lives and it was deeply unnerving for the both us.

In fact, the phone call scared me and Tina so much that, even though we had only just moved house, we decided that it was better to be safe than sorry, and we made arrangements to travel to Kent and start looking for another rented house, away from the scene of this latest trauma. The trail, we hoped and prayed, would end at the Norwich house. None of the telephone numbers would move with us and a forwarding address would be given to the landlord only, not to the postal service. The next property we would rent would not be listed on the electoral role for at least a year, to ensure that the track would go cold for whichever radical organisation may have been trying to trace survivors. We would do all we could to put obstacles in their path.

Thankfully, we found a house in Maidstone, Kent, that was conveniently situated on a very busy main road, which would ensure the likelihood of many witnesses if something should go down at any time. There was a clear view of the main road and surrounding properties from the

front door, so we could see who was coming and going easily. Also, if there was a car waiting or suspicious characters lurking in the vicinity, our getaway would be very open and easy. The landlady was discreet and co-operative too, which was a big help.

Before all the nonsense, I had been looking forward to moving up to Norwich. The people had always been friendly and talkative and I loved that area. We had hoped that getting away from the rat race in London would finally start the healing process for us both and that the many birds, small boats and the charming windmills that peppered the countryside would provide comforting surroundings. I definitely thought that Norwich would give us the quieter, uneventful life we so desperately needed.

Now, once again, we were faced with a forced move, under undesirable circumstances. The crazy day arrived when we had to uproot and, oh my goodness, what a madhouse! I had organised the boxes and moving items to the truck. Once everything was packed up, I gave the removal men cash and a drink so they could get on their way. I planned to catch up later, once I had cleaned the house and posted the keys back through the letterbox.

A few hours later I was ready to leave. I called the landlord and loaded the doggies into the car in the only available space, which was on the front seat. I put them in the pet carrier and called Tina at work to let her know that the house had been closed up and that everything was done and dusted. 'I'll see you at the new house,' I said.

'Drive carefully won't you,' she replied. 'Love you.' She

had to complete her full working day before she could set out on the long drive on snowy roads from Norfolk to Kent.

My own journey was uneventful, except for a nature break for the doggies and myself, and we sailed along the motorway, as we had left at just the right time in between the morning and evening rush hours.

A few hours later I pulled into the driveway of our new home on Loose Road under the watchful eyes of the neighbours – a married couple with three children: two boys and a girl, who was the eldest. How I prayed that this would be our safe haven, where we could settle back down to a more normal life.

I opened the front door and, as soon as I walked into the house, I felt a peace wash over me. I walked the doggies through to the enclosed back garden and let them out of the pet carrier. They romped in the snow and little Beelie, being a Teacup Yorkie, disappeared underneath the snow, then jumped up to check where she was in relation to the new house. It was as big an adventure for them as it was for me and Tina – the high-pitched barks that filled the garden said it all.

Then I called them inside after a while and phoned the removal guys to see where they were. They informed me they would come to unload on the following morning, as, now it was after 9pm, it was far too late to be moving in. We arranged a time of 8.30am.

In the meantime, as Tina hadn't arrived yet, I bought fish and chips from the chippie down the road and, boy, they were delicious! After eating, I made up our makeshift camp

beds in our new bedroom and waited for Tina's arrival, counting down the minutes until I saw her car pull up outside and I knew that she was safe.

Although I settled into our new home in Maidstone really well, the sexual-abuse nightmare with the creepy man continued, only now I was dreaming of armies of other men who were abusing me too. I had been having disturbing nightmares and the usual broken sleep for months but it all seemed to get worse after we moved to Kent, maybe because of the change I was, yet again, having to cope with. It was like dark beings rising up from the underworld, to haunt me about a past I had long buried.

In my dreams, I was always fighting men off, kicking and screaming. There was a sinister feel to the images I was seeing as I relived the abuse over and over – men with no clear faces, hunting innocence and laughing at my pleas for them to stop. I knew that I had to somehow get a grip but how on earth can you stop nightmares that you know are really memories of the truth?

You can't.

CHAPTER ELEVEN

SAVING MY FACE IN THAILAND

In the aftermath of 7 July 2005, the doctors and other medical professionals were rather overwhelmed by the amount of medical attention required by survivors and the bereaved. There was a lot of legal wrangling to obtain compensation from the government for our horrific injuries and for the families who had lost a loved one. I had complained to the government – as had other survivors – that the then compensation system in the UK was overly bureaucratic and too slow in providing for our needs. I still look back and thank God that we had the assistance of the International Red Cross in the early days – it was this organisation that paid for the dental work to repair my jaw and get rid of all the poisons that were in my jaw and teeth cavities.

I was one of just 90 survivors to be given a small interim payment as the investigations into my injuries continued.

The Criminal Injuries Compensation Authority (CICA) were unable to define an award for me until after my initial surgeries had been completed, which was frustrating and depressing. The more bomb victims I spoke to, the more I recognised that there was such an injustice to the system. We had paid – some with their lives – for the terrorist attack on our country and we deserved to be fully compensated as quickly as was possible.

As I saw it, my mission was to get healed as best I could in as short a period of time and to help other survivors in any way that I possibly could. I've been a fighter all my life, so there was nothing new in having to fight for what I believed to be right. Even though I was experiencing major injuries and emotional problems myself, I felt that I had to make my mark and be the voice for the victims who didn't have a voice of their own.

An organisation had been set up by the Red Cross and Ken Livingstone called the London Bombings Charitable Relief Fund. It raised millions of pounds from well-wishers and all donations went to the bomb victims and their families to help pay for their medical bills and any other monetary problems they may have experienced. It was an amazing charity and it helped to fill in the cracks left by the CICA, so that people at least got some compensation to help them to recover and heal.

In March 2006 I received a phone call from the Greater London Assembly to ask me to provide crucial witness evidence, as the London Mayor's Office was holding its own review into the events of the previous year. I was invited to speak as one of the 7/7 survivors at a huge

meeting and I agreed, although it took every ounce of strength I had to agree to go public with everything I remembered and had suffered.

A few nights before the event at the London City Hall, my nervous system felt like it was being rewired – or short circuiting. As I have dysphasia – a language disorder caused by the brain damage – it was important to prepare for the event lest I stumbled over my words, created unusual spoonerisms, or generally had my train of thought disrupted. I prepared a week before and wrote my cue cards out using the thickest black marker pen that I could find. I practised and practised hard, because I knew that this was my chance to really make an impact.

Some of the pieces of information from the day of the bombings that I had mentally collected since it happened started to come together as I sat at home preparing my speech. So that I could offer my observations of the day, I had to force myself to look at it as an impartial bystander and report on my experiences. At the time, I couldn't help thinking that everything was about to change. I wonder sometimes how we, as human beings, can endure the rise in intensity within our lives when faced with such a traumatic event. But, somehow, we do.

I knew that the whole of March, and certainly the seven days that flank the Equinox either side, would be an intense emotional roller coaster for me – that seems an understatement now! In an odd sort of a way, I felt more sensitive and in touch with the world. Retracing the darkest hours from the 7 July bombings with other survivors did make me wonder if I could relive the

memories for the London Assembly Resilience review and hold it all together for that short period of time. It was going to be an enormous challenge and, in my darkest hours, I feared failure. But something inside me willed me on to do it.

The day of the private inquiry in London came and I met with Councillor Richard Barnes, who went on to become the Deputy Mayor of London and a firm friend. Many of the people I spoke to on the day over the initial tea were full of practical suggestions on how to improve the response to the aftermath of the disaster, continually stressing their desire for a public inquiry. I held the testimony together, stating the situation as matter-of-factly as I could, but then I lost it at the end because I was so emotional. I couldn't close off as the tears rolled down my cheeks. Councillor Richard Barnes realised the emotional pain I was in and he closed my statement for me.

After the inquiry, a group of us got together and we called ourselves 'The Survivor's Coalition'. In the days and weeks that followed the terrorist attacks, many survivors were left alone, feeling traumatised and isolated. I used the Family Assistance Centre, which was set up in Victoria after the bombings, only once. The name had misled a lot of people, who thought it was really only for helping the families of the dead and talking to other survivors. We really felt that there was the need to form a group specifically for anyone who had been affected in any way by the bombings.

I called the Scrutiny Manager of the Greater London Assembly, Janet Hughes, to find out about the committee

and the planned special 'scrutiny' meetings. I was told that there was an open meeting on 23 March 2006 between 10am and 1pm and they would be pleased for me to go along to give my own accounts of that day. Initially, the time slot was set for the 'experiences of the bereaved' but the descriptive name of our group's contributors was later changed to the '7/7 Panel of Survivors'. Later still it became known as the 'Magnificent Seven', referring to the key survivors chosen to discuss and give evidence of our own experiences of the incident. I was one of them and it was an incredible and humbling experience to be part of that hearing, together with so many other people who had suffered as I had. I gained strength from being with them because we all wanted the truth about what had happened that day.

At the same time, I had pursued the possibility of a class action on behalf of all the survivors and the bereaved. I hired a restorative-justice solicitor in London in a practice famous for gaining compensation for people after the Lockerbie plane crash: H2O Law. We had researched the various avenues to pursue and looked at the options, including the costs of the suit and in which country the case would be brought – either the USA or the UK. The information that was researched into regarding who was behind the bombings and how much training they had received, was leading back to a single point, and also a specific bank was highlighted. The case gained evidence fast but, in the end, we were one key aspect short. We needed a USA national with an American passport to be part of the class action to give us enough evidence to make

our case – it was all very complicated legally. In the UK we couldn't find anyone who could back us financially, so it was suggested that we find an American victim to join the class action. That way, it could be heard in the US where we might have had a bigger chance of finding someone to stump-up the money for legal costs. We were clutching at straws a little bit, but we really thought we might have a chance. For years we traced survivors to Queens, New York across to two girls in Canada and various others, but to no avail. The case remains open, waiting for a survivor in the USA to come forward and agree to join the cause. Until then, everything is on hold.

While all this was going on, I still desperately needed surgery to repair my face and to help me to swallow again properly. The NHS route to the surgical procedures was a very slow process and just as demoralising as when I had waited for appointments with doctors and specialists to come through for me.

In November 2006 Tina and I were invited to attend a personal, private presentation in London by Thailand's internationally renowned Professor Surapong Ambhanwong, President of the Thai Private Hospital Association and the Chief Medical and International Business Officer at Phyathai. The event was hosted near the River Thames and featured the world's most influential people in their respective fields, there to talk about the most recent advancements in medical technology and medical tourism.

We were both equally impressed with what Thailand had to offer me. The doctors who worked with Professor Surapong were Thai and they had trained extensively in

Boston, USA and in Europe, gaining a great deal of medical expertise. They had perfect manners and they spoke fluent English, which was obviously extremely important as far as I was concerned. It seemed that they could repair my face and my swallow reflex in two weeks – so it would be a bit like going on holiday with surgery in between the relaxing parts. I read that, by travelling abroad for surgery to somewhere exotic, where there is sunshine and the facilities for proper relaxation, this could actually aid recovery time, providing, of course, that the surgeons and the hospital were completely trained and equipped in every aspect of the surgical process. I also read some horror stories from women who had gone abroad for cosmetic surgery, which had nearly always ended badly because of unqualified doctors who claimed to be plastic surgeons, who very clearly were not specialised in the field at all.

The overall price tag for the surgery to repair my face, the travel, hotel expenses and the aftercare was going to be £25,000, and I would have to pay for it upfront. The Criminal Injuries Compensation Authority was not giving out any payments until after people had had their surgeries and, in the end, I was awarded £12,500 towards it, just about half the amount. I had to be thankful for small mercies though, because many of the victims got as little as 25 per cent towards the cost of their surgeries and to help with recovery costs. I still think that the amounts given were insulting when you think about what we all went through.

Tina and I agreed that, in order to speed up my recovery and to possibly help with the PTSD, Thailand was a must.

We did lots of research into the hospital over there and the type of care patients were given and we discovered that the Thai doctors are perfectionists who pride themselves on clean hospitals, brilliant aftercare and, in general, providing the best medical care possible. We had savings, so could afford to pay the £25,000 for the operation at the Phyathai Hospital in Bangkok. This is the hospital where Professor Surapong was based and had, in 2006, decided to open an international ward. As I was going to be one of the first 'ferang' or foreign patients to use the new ward, Dr Surapong had me and Tina send him a long list of all the services that we thought were necessary, so that we could decide whether to use the medical services for all of my treatments, or just some of them.

For us, it was important that the hospital had full-cycle transportation services for every part of the trip, from disembarking the plane to getting to the hotel, then to the hospital and back to the hotel. We needed to know that hospital personnel would be able to arrange our flights and visas and escort us through customs checks at the airport, since neither of us can speak Thai. We also reviewed the private-nursing situation and how long a nurse would be assigned to us, what the response time would be after hours, should anything go wrong following the operation, and lastly what the discharge procedure was for the convalescence stay in Hua Hin, a little town three hours from the hospital. Hua Hin – meaning 'stone head' – is situated on the coastline, and it was agreed that my medical information would also be sent to their local hospital should I need any treatment while I was there.

To reduce the tension of the trip and to make it easier for me to be able to eat and feel at home, the international division at the hospital agreed on a menu for me beforehand. This included good old Twining's Breakfast tea, fish and chips, roast chicken with all the trimmings as part of a Sunday dinner and even English chocolate. It was a very English menu and, long after I had left, it was kept for other British patients and also for the Scottish and Welsh patients. For the Irish, they added a variety of potatoes, including potato cakes at breakfast. I am sure there were some very happy patients as a result of those menus, and I was pleased to be a part of getting those food plans put together.

My surgery was booked in for the spring of 2007. Tina and I had a good flight out, even though it was at least 12 hours long, but I was more excited than impatient to get to Bangkok. After having consulted with Professor Surapong several times over the phone, I knew in my heart of hearts that this was the best thing I could be doing at that time. I was ready for my face to be pieced back together, ready to look in the mirror and see the real Beverli, not just the ghost that I had become since the bombings. I wanted the old 'me' back, and that long journey was to start with my face.

At the time, I didn't know how much money the CICA were going to be paying me towards the cost of the trip but both Tina and I agreed that, even if we didn't get a penny, we had to go and, if it used up all of our little nest egg, it had to be that way. After the bombings, we lived very much in the moment, rather than planning for the future,

since it was glaringly apparent that in one day your life could be changed forever. We decided that, although, like every human being, we never know what's around the corner, at least we could plan for something that was going to help me live a better, everyday life, and anything that did that was going to be worth the money.

We were met, as promised, at Bangkok International Airport by a hospital interpreter and taken directly to the hospital. Dr Surapong came to see me on the first day and then again after I'd had several tests to assess my overall condition, to make sure I was healthy enough for the surgery.

'I think that all the stress that you have been under, coupled with the exposure to toxins held within the smoke after the tube explosion, has had a huge impact on your immune system,' he said. 'Your immune system isn't functioning properly, so it's no wonder you feel ill all the time.' He told me that, when I got back to the UK, I had to talk more to friends and family, spend time doing fun things and that, when I was feeling sad or stressed, I should talk about it, rather than bottle it up. 'This will reduce the burden,' he said wisely. 'It will make you feel at peace knowing that there is someone out there who cares because buried emotions and thoughts can increase your medical problems.'

His words touched me and made me sit up and listen. Of course, it was no wonder that I was taking so much time to heal and to get my PTSD under control – I realised that the only way to move forward after the surgeries was to somehow accept the past and move forward in a positive

way. That's easier said than done but at least it was a step in the right direction!

Recovery after the surgical procedures was my number-one concern, especially following the oral surgery. When I came round, my face was so swollen and bruised that it looked like I had been involved in a major car accident – I was not a pretty sight. I was really worried about the risk of infection at the surgical site so, when I was transferred to our studio in Hua Hin, Tina made sure that we followed all the surgeon's instructions about aftercare as best we could. As soon as we arrived there I knew it was the perfect place to convalesce. Our studio overlooked vast parklands and it was very modern, to deal with our European needs! The en-suite bathroom was a walk-in 'wet room' with a small window that opened onto a beautiful coconut tree laden with dozens of coconuts in reach of the window. It was funny – during the night, we would be woken up by a thudding sound just outside the shower and, in the morning, there would be several coconuts on the ground ready for us to pick up and drink the milk from.

Our bedroom was finished with natural fabrics and calming hues. There was a lot of white, which was soothing on the eye and the soul. Our curtains opened onto a large, sweeping balcony, where Tina and I would eat our breakfast at a small round table overlooking the estate. It was so very quiet and tranquil. Staff would bring us all our meals there for the first few days, then we would join other patients in a gloriously grand dining room. For those first days I didn't think it would be fair on anyone else if I was to walk around covered in bandages – what a sight I was!

I was told that I had to keep my head elevated by pillows but, in fact, that was the only way I could lie anyway because it was too painful to lie flat. If I did, the thudding in my head would start and the ringing of blood gushing into my ears was so painful that I couldn't sleep anyway. When I got this throbbing pain, I had to sit up in bed and prop myself upright against the headboard and find a spot where the pillows didn't touch my head and where my jaws and cheeks were free from the pressure of the pillow. I had a large selection of ice packs to apply to different parts of my face as and when I needed them. My face, neck and shoulders were very stiff. This continued for about 10 days but I was told that this was normal.

I was expecting a lot of pain after the oral surgery, particularly because of the amount of work that had been carried out. The internal stitches in my mouth had very long suture ends, which were uncomfortable, although it didn't take me long to get used to them. My tongue constantly had a mind of its own, feeling the edges of the stitches and wiggling them about! I thought about cutting them off myself but then decided against it in case I messed up what the doctors had done. The dental surgeon had prescribed me some amazing pain medication and I had to clean my mouth out at least three times a day with a special antibiotic, to help prevent infections setting in.

After just a few days I started to feel better. The beautiful surroundings truly helped and I was desperate to get up and about to have a look around. The hospital had laid on special activities for patients and their families for when they started to feel better. Tina and I did a Thai-cooking

class and we were taught to cook basic, traditional Thai meals on tables under the coconut groves. It was one of the most enjoyable experiences I've had and, to this day, we can both remember how to cook those dishes. We also spent a day on the beach towards the end of the trip. I donned a big beach hat and large sunglasses and Tina and I sat under an umbrella all day, letting the warm sun soak into our bodies while we listened to the gentle lap of the ocean waves. It was so peaceful – I could have stayed right there forever.

On the last day, we managed a trip out to one of the local shopping malls but, really, that was a bit of a mistake because just getting there was difficult for me. Even though our driver drove very carefully over the numerous bumps in the roads, every little shock in the car that caused my body to move resulted in severe pain in my face, neck and shoulders. Still, I was glad that we made the effort and had a little look at the mall.

The Thai people believe that a key part of the healing process is to focus on emotional problems from deep within and I was assigned a specialist psychoanalyst to review the status and progression of my severe PTSD. I went to a few sessions to evaluate my mental state and general wellbeing and I was prescribed several alternative therapies. One in particular stands out in my mind. After a particularly intensive meeting, I was sent to a spa for a two-hour healing-therapy session, which started with a special 'mud sleep' using the famous Din Saw Pong, which is white mud.

I was covered in a light-coloured detoxifying mud and

then I was splattered with a different, warm mud, infused with a variety of herbs and essential oils. It took me an absolute age to relax because I had to be completely naked for the treatment, which is not something I wanted to do, particularly with the memories of my childhood never far from my mind. But the Thai ladies were very warm and safe and, above all, gentle. 'You have beautiful white skin,' one of them said with a lovely smile, and this was a huge complement because, in Thai culture, having snow-white skin is seen as a sign of great beauty.

After I had been covered in the mud, I was wrapped in a type of 'Clingfilm' and propped up on a few towels on a table covered with more warm towels. As I lay there, they dimmed the lights and I fell asleep to gentle monastic chants. Oh my goodness, it was wonderful. I think it was the first time in months that I fell asleep quickly and easily.

When I woke up, I was unwrapped by the beautiful, angelic Thai ladies and led to a shower to wash off of all the mud, then I was given a towel, a robe and slippers made from grass. I was shown into another room, where the oil-and-massage therapy would continue. There, for the first time in my life, I allowed someone close to my body because I wanted them to be there, not because they were going to be near to me anyway, regardless of my wishes. I had never let anyone massage me deeply before because the memories of the past had created an extreme barrier and gave me an overwhelming need to scream and run. I was so fragile yet, in Thailand, I was relaxed and calm as I felt the women's gentle hands touching my body

while music from Wat, the Buddhist temple, was piped into the room.

During the trip, I was also blessed with spending a special day with the monks in the main Buddhist monastery in Hua Hin. Through an interpreter, I asked them, why me? Why had I seen so much horror in my life? It was a burning question that I often thought about and could never find an answer to. I mean, being severely sexually abused as a child is an absolutely terrible thing for anyone to have to endure. But then to almost die in a terrorist attack and be left with horrific injuries on top of all that hurt and shame, is just beyond belief. I had been struggling with this issue ever since the bombings, and part of me thought I must have been a bad person in a previous life, or something equally as dramatic. But the monks told me that there was a karmic pattern that had opened up for me that would lead to my full recovery.

Two weeks after the surgery, we were back on the plane on our way home. A big part of me didn't want to go back to the very place where all those memories lurked. Even though I only stayed in Thailand for a short period of time, I had grown to love it. The people were so kind and soothing and the care that I received from everyone involved with my surgery and aftercare couldn't be faulted.

I think that going to Thailand was definitely the right thing to have done, and it was there that I truly started the healing process, not just physically but mentally too. I went home a much calmer person with a better sense of worth and a deep-rooted determination to live my life as fully as possible without letting my demons interrupt my plans too

much. I knew it was going to be a hard road ahead but my strength was definitely coming back to me, particularly emotionally, and it was when I got home that I decided that I would take up the reins – literally – and get back to doing something I had loved all my life: the horses. If anything could help me in my recovery – and keep me there – I knew that horses could and I was ready to welcome them back into my life.

CHAPTER TWELVE

BACK IN
THE SADDLE

When I got back from Thailand, I was filled with a new-found hope for my future. Even though I was still recovering physically from the surgeries, mentally I had never been in a better place since the bombings.

While I was overseas, I had begun to think about horses again and how, up until then, I had generally always had a horse in my life. As I looked back on my life during quiet periods of reflection when I was alone in the living room having a read, or when Tina was at work, I remembered how, during every traumatic event in my life, I had always had a horse to help pull me through.

I thought back to how Humbug, my first horse, made my life bearable during my childhood. For all the times that I was sexually abused by Peter and his sick, perverted cronies, I could always cry on my horse's shoulder, knowing that he would never judge me or hold what was

going on against me. He was my confidante, my piece of fun and my best friend all rolled into one big furry pony and, to this day, I dread to think what may have happened to me if I hadn't had him to ease the pain I suffered on a daily basis. Just by standing with him in his stable, Humbug had the knack of making me feel that everything was really going to be all right and that the bad times would pass. His love definitely gave me the will to carry on.

My dedication to horses had always been a priority for me because I believe that you get back what you put into any relationship. In the past, I have broken relationships with lovers and friends if they didn't understand – or at least try to understand – the feeling and place of importance that horses have in my heart and my soul. Now I was going through an absolute nightmare and a mountain of feelings and, for the first time in my life, I didn't have a horse to turn to for comfort.

A friend told me about Equine Assisted Therapy in the UK because she thought it might be something that I would enjoy, knowing of my deep love for horses. I read up on it and it certainly looked like something that would help me. Basically, Equine Assisted Therapy was set up in Norfolk in 1990 by a lady called Ruth McMahon, a senior occupational therapist, after she recognised the incredible changes in her patients' mental health after spending time with horses.

She saw that, with regular contact with horses, patients gained more self-esteem and inter-personal skills, some patients became more outgoing and talkative and some autistic children began to communicate spontaneously

with their families for the first time. The horses seemed to help patients overcome their fears, build up trust, respect and compassion, and generally helped to develop coping techniques that they could use in their everyday lives.

At the time, even though when I felt up to it I was back to work here and there as a consultant analyst and earning good money again, I was still suffering from balance problems and I was taking 16 different tablets just to get me out of bed in the mornings and to be able to function. I was taking a variety of meds, including Stemetil, along with other tablets that, taken together, assist with balance. With the balance issues, I knew that getting on a horse again wasn't going to be the easiest thing in the world, but I was desperate to give it a try.

The next time I went to see my GP, I asked him about getting back on a horse. 'Absolutely not!' was his answer. 'Beverli, it is highly unlikely that you will be able to ride again. It is inadvisable, as sustaining a fall from a horse could cause considerable health issues!'

Now, I can be extremely stubborn when I want to be and I was angry with my GP for shooting down my plans, so I thought that, if I spoke with my neurologist at the hospital, he would know enough to be able to recognise how helpful Equine Assisted Therapy could be for me. I wasn't prepared for what he had to say either.

'Under no circumstances are you to even think about getting a horse,' the consultant said, and he looked at me as if he thought I was quite stupid for thinking of doing such a dangerous thing. 'You have severe balance issues,which means that you could fall off the horse very

easily. Taking a fall will add to you heath issues.' He looked at me kindly for a minute as I took it all in, tears starting to well up in my eyes. 'I am sorry,' he continued,' but I don't advise returning to horse riding at this stage of your recovery!'

'But I think it could help me come to terms with what's happened to me,' I argued, not meaning to question the good doctor quite so aggressively when he was the expert but, for my own piece of mind, I had to put my thoughts and opinions to him. 'Riding a horse would give me back my sense of worth and it could even help me to learn to balance again. I've read all about it. I've ridden horses all of my life and I am a good rider. I know I can do this, embrace larger horizons, more possibilities.'

'Beverli, with your situation right now, you just can't risk a fall,' my neurologist said. 'I am really sorry, there are too many risks. I wouldn't be responsible or a good doctor if I didn't advise you against it.'

I was devastated when I went home that day because I knew that getting back on a horse was the best thing for me to do. I couldn't accept what my neurologist had told me – he might as well have told me to curl up in a box and wait to die if I couldn't ride, because that's how much getting back on a horse meant to me. When I got home that same evening, I told Tina what had been said and, initially, I think that she was secretly pleased that this idea of mine had been botched by not just one, but two, doctors. Seeing me so upset was hard for her though because, from the moment we met, she was aware of my life-time love for horses.

When we talked, she said, 'Honey, whatever your

situation, just enjoy everything about it and learn to take just exactly enough from life.' Forever the wise woman, she had seen the pain first hand, caring for me and expecting nothing from me.

Before she met me, Tina liked horses but she was quite simply terrified of them. As a very young child, she had been out riding with her favourite uncle, Phil, when the stroppy gold-coloured Welsh Cob mare that she was riding bolted for home at the first opportunity, with Tina screaming for help on her back. That experience had scarred her for life and understandably so but, when we met, I was very keen for her to share my passion and I give her credit, she did eventually come round to spending time at the barn with me and my horse Three Times My Lady, an Appaloosa mare with strong Quarter-horse lines, I'm a Doc a Lena and other champion lines.

The horses loved her too and, gradually, she began to enjoy being nibbled and groomed by them almost as much as I did. They would nuzzle and whinny whenever they heard her footsteps, as if they were giving her a familiar and very personal greeting. It was as if they knew that this person was very special to me and, therefore, special to them too. So through spending quality time with the horses and knowing how much good they can do, Tina knew in her heart that I wouldn't give up riding for the rest of my life. I had often said that, if I couldn't ride or be around horses, what was the point of living at all. And just before the bombings I had been thinking about buying a horse again, so she knew this was something I wanted really badly.

I am not a quitter and I was determined to find a way to alleviate my symptoms and discover a coping strategy and a daily management plan to deal effectively with my health problems. I needed to think about the facts, what I saw and experienced, and how that made me feel, and my reactions. I needed to face the truth. Whatever form of counselling I was getting, was I really ready to move on and begin the process of evolution?

I sure was!

It seemed I was the everlasting survivor. For years I was trapped by the events of the past, a double whammy: the bombings of 7/7 and Child Sex Abuse – bloody charming! Not one for half measures, I needed to learn about my psyche and how to treat myself right in order to heal to get out of being in 'survivor limbo' and to move away from being a survivor for ever.

So I chose life and I continue to choose life on all levels. I made an active choice to continue to live and grow, to learn and to make peace with my tortured soul.

For a long time I kept telling myself, 'It wasn't your fault, you're not to blame.' Those words brought emotional pain with them as I tried hard to convince myself that the survivor's guilt I was feeling was wrong and unnecessary. But I still felt it. The counsellor I was seeing couldn't get me past the guilt of surviving both traumas, even though they were years and years apart. I remained in pain, even though everyone I knew, including my therapists, were all trying to tell me that my suffering was not my fault.

I reached a point at St Bartholomew's Hospital in

London when I couldn't continue my sessions. There had been no forward movement for weeks. The clinician discussed the possibility of direct hospital treatment with the help of drugs for a period of four weeks. That didn't seem right either. A fellow passenger, Veronica, who had been caught up in 7/7 and who became a really good friend, had agreed to the same therapy but, in her case, she was to remain in hospital for eight weeks. She was traumatised and kept in an almost prison-like ward with bars on the windows. She felt no major relief or benefit. Based on her experience and my gut feeling that the treatment wouldn't be right for me, I decided to seek therapy elsewhere.

My personal opinion was that therapists, psychologists and councillors were unable to change my feelings. I just didn't feel like a traditional victim – I felt that there was a degree of 'gain' associated with what had happened to me. That is to say that I did get something out of the years of abuse I suffered, just as I gained out of recovering from 7/7. Not financially but emotionally, there was a gain and, in some way, a secondary gain: for the abuse, I got to stay in the home and I had a horse, nice clothes and plenty of attention – often I was the centre of attention. Ah, there was the secondary gain!

I was not prepared to play the 'victim game'. I know I was young – in some cases, very young – and too weak to defend myself but, somewhere inside, I know that I could have created a tantrum, screamed, bitten, kicked and created a scene. I didn't.

In fact I should have made more of the popping to the

bathroom, being caught short more than I was, instead of going to the toilet in the men's houses. I should have vomited more in the back seat of the car more regularly than I did. I recall that the abuse stopped for a while after the 'vomit' car rides and the pee-stained carpets, beds or sofas. I was not in favour for a time after those incidents. 'Should', I guess, is the wrong word to use. I should use 'could'. I *could* have, yet I chose not to.

It's too easy to agree that it wasn't my fault. There was pressure put on me to accept that it wasn't my fault but that didn't feel right.

I believe that I had a choice and I chose to accept the secondary gain. Just exactly what the secondary gain was and how it came about and how I experienced that gain, I've yet to flesh out totally as I continue my journey. Tenacious as all hell, not easily shaken off, much like a possessive dog with a bone, I will keep going until I find answers.

I'm being deeply honest with myself, looking at the raw facts in a calm and tranquil environment and the inner 'me' looks better from plodding along on the back of a horse. Accepting myself with all my weaknesses is much easier when confronted with the unconditional and non-judgemental love of a horse. Horses show, in their own way, that, for them, everyone counts, everyone is the same and everyone deserves a second chance, free from the stigma of past mistakes, no matter what.

So I *knew* that, looking back on my childhood, I had the choice to fight back or not to fight back. The small inner voice – the Jiminy Cricket of the Pinocchio story – sitting

on my shoulder and chirping, told me that what was happening was not quite right, even though I felt a degree of 'trust' for the people involved and trust in Peter as a 'father figure'. Somehow, I had known it was wrong, yet I didn't fight back. I chose to comply, to not make a scene, be a good girl, even though a needy girl. I bought into the pathetic helpless game – the game of the victim.

So no more games. Not ever!

I had to reach a point within me where I could accept myself; accept that I did have a choice and accept that I made my choice and lived with its severe consequences. My next step was then to dissect what had happened and begin a difficult level of scrutiny towards absolution. I wanted to confront the feelings of guilt, shame, sexuality and fear without having to hide away from everyday life and distorting my view further.

During a session defined as review of my TBI (traumatic brain injury – my head injury that occurred during the 7/7 incident) I discovered that I had bruised brain tissue. At the same session, we also discussed the secondary damage: swollen face and head, raised temperature but no fever, various imbalances. I felt that, as I had been discharged from King's College Hospital Neurology Department, I could open a line of discussion regarding horse riding and my return to the sport. I assured my doctor that the tablets were working and that I felt it was time to work on my mobility issues and my lack of balance.

I spoke softly and carefully, thinking about the words I had rehearsed before arriving at the appointment with my GP. She was her usual understanding self, injecting humour

now and then into the conversation. She – perhaps under-standably – wasn't comfortable with my expected return to the sport; I could see in her face that she was finding it hard to accept what I was proposing.

She made the point that, if I couldn't even get up and down the stairs without holding on to the banister, how did I propose to stay upright on a horse without slipping off, as balance seemed to be an integral part of horse riding? I joked that I would have a very small horse that was close to the ground, so it would be less height to fall from! Not so funny – no laugh at all from my GP, nor even a glimmer of a smile.

I told her that I was at peace and most comfortable when I was at the yard, working with the horses; that I was able to make a mental detour when I was mounted, even if we were just walking around the arena or the outdoor school, or perhaps on a short outdoor hack around the property – I connected with myself.

My doctor realised that I was going to start up riding again whether she liked it or not and she cautioned me, going through my health conditions and making me aware of the risks.

Two words come to mind: 'deaf' and 'ears'. I was driven instinctively. I knew that horses would help me more than 'talking therapy' or the 'freeing of emotions' techniques I had heard about. I had made my decision.

I woke up the next morning feeling good and excited. I was slightly nervous as well but I knew that the pain I would experience from riding again would be part of the healing process

As I had treated myself to a four-legged friend using some of my savings, I felt that settling to use her as simply a 'therapy horse' was lying to myself. So I had to come to terms with the fact that my blonde bombshell, Barely Whizable, was a bit on the small side for me, measuring at a little under 15hh – more like 14.3hh. I am 90 per cent legs, a tall, leggy 5ft, 8in (1.80m in new money)! On Whizzi I was all legs, riding along with my feet way past her knees. I looked like a sloppy, under-horsed rider, as if I was on a pony.

I approached a well-known international horse dealer and appraiser, who worked in both Canada and the USA, with a view to her finding me a suitable horse that I could ride and use as a therapy horse. And so Audra Ballean of Twin Creeks started the search for a mare. She would write me a daily report of her findings and send photographs as well as DVD or links to videos on YouTube, so that I could watch the horses being put through their paces and, where horses had been utilised for therapy for the disabled, view the relevant video footage.

Audra also sent through a package with DVDs that had been made by the sellers, showing their horses being tacked up and doing both Showing and Ridden classes as well as trail and horsemanship.

There were no horses in the UK or mainland Europe of the calibre that I required at the time. I had looked for a good few months. I had gone across to Monchengladbach and also to Austria to view and ride a mare that was a little on the young side but had a good mind and a kind nature. She was quite lovely but had a terrible stable manner about

her; she was fiercely territorial and pinned her ears back on her head, especially when she was given her food – she would scowl and then turn her hindquarters towards you in a threatening manner. She did behave nicely, however, when she was being ridden and when she was groomed.

Another little mare I flew to see was in Germany. She was very pretty also, a brown-and-white horse (of a breed known as a 'Paint') with a strong Quarter-horse blood line. She was a really devoted 'wind-sucker' which means that she would grip onto an object and suck wind into her stomach. Even though she wore a crib collar, which is a piece of leather buckled around her throat to try to stop her sucking in, she was still able to suck in wind. The vet said that her teeth had been ground down and that the cribbing, potentially, could become a major health issue.

I added those requirements to the list for Audra – no vices, no cribbing or wind-sucking, no kicking or biting or aggression, no illnesses or long-term health conditions – as well as a firm list of wants.

In the end, I bought Chips Tommy Girl without even riding her. I relied totally on the video and DVD as well as the personal ride of the agent that I'd hired to find me the perfect pleasure horse.

I had spoken to the Ministry of Agriculture, Fisheries and Food (as it then was) about the importation rules for horses being brought into the UK from the USA and I was told that the one-month quarantine with weekly blood tests, with the horse kept in total isolation from other horses, was not negotiable. 'Sneeze trays' between the stalls

and surrounding areas were a must to halt any cross-contamination between horses waiting to leave or enter the country. All paperwork had to be in order and stamped by the relative authorities. I commissioned John Parker International Equine Transport to help me, so that I didn't have to go through updating faxes and negotiating the paperwork for the import. They had brought in my reining mare very successfully and with no injury, so I commissioned them to bring Tommy Girl for me. There were two possible flights, one via Luxembourg and the other via Amsterdam. The company booked the Luxembourg trip for Tommy Girl, as they had a large float of 16 horses going in and coming back, since they were taking a full team and we would just take up a travelling stall that was free on the return journey. John Parker had a large network of stalls for the evening sleep across Europe, and the EU rules carefully governed the time that the drivers could truck the horses as a total of eight hours – no more. The horses were then unloaded and taken into stalls with big beds of straw or shavings so they could lie down and have a good night's sleep after a meal of hay mixed with Haylage (a grass crop that is cut, harvested and stored to feed farm animals) in large hay nets or, in some cases, piled in the corner of a hay bar.

When Tommy Girl arrived and walked off the international transport after three days trucking across mainland Europe, I immediately fell in love with the horse. Tina fell for Tommy too.

I had entered Tommy Girl into a national show, which took place about a month after she arrived in England.

However, because she was bumped off her first flight and then left a week later, she arrived over 11 days after the date that she should have, so, in fact, two weeks of our show training schedule was missed. I had a mere fortnight to get her into fitness and show condition. It was quite hectic, so I kept her arrival and her background in shows – especially Pleasure and Trail showmanship – a bit of a secret. As I had purchased a Rolls Royce of a horse I wasn't even riding at Morris Minor level! How embarrassing. The lady who had owned Tommy Girl before me – the mother of a mother-and-daughter team from Hunter Hill Stables – had said that she would come to the UK and ride her for me in the shows, especially in the European shows, like the Celebration and other 'Festival of Colour' classes. I was about to make a star. I entered the Trail class as a junior-rank novice and also the Western Pleasure novice class. I won the Pleasure class but was DQ'd (or disqualified) in the Trail class, a video of which remains on YouTube under 'Beverli and Tommy', where the mistakes are there for all to see.

The errors and the DQ didn't matter to me, as I had entered in spite of my fear and nervousness and also against doctor's orders. I had entered and won. My trainer had entered Tommy Girl in the Open classes and she won, beating all the American Quarter horses. It was the NSBA (The National Snaffle Bit Association) class, so the plaque came with a small purse of winnings. My true 'winnings' was me – I had won against the greatest odds. No one really knew just how much the entire event had meant to me. The whole day was a total dream come true and

changed my life entirely. I knew that Tommy was going to always look after me and that she was going to heal my soul. She kept me safe.

When it comes to horses, there is always something new to learn and experience, even if your life is overcomplicated and crammed full of issues! Through the years, I have been saved from too much introspection by my horses. At some points, I was a danger to myself. Perhaps others didn't see the danger but I always knew it was there. I was often close to boiling and it was horses that brought me back from the brink of explosion. In a calm and loving way, the horses would show me their side of life, speaking in a unique way – a hidden horse language – sharing their horse-herd community and friendship with me. There is a truth that only horses can share.

My horses seemed to mirror what I was feeling at the time. If they put in a buck now and then, or all on the same day during a training session, I was forced to have a good look at why they may be 'hind feet in the air' – what were they trying to tell me? If they were lethargic and sad, the 'mirror' was facing right back at me. In a way, each horse was just right for me at the right time in my life. With Humbug, I needed that older, calmer, understanding horse; one with a capability for gentle reflection – one that could zero in on my soul, undertake more listening and cuddling than anything. Looking after me on a hack and keeping me safe was the job at hand.

My heart's desire has been centred on horses for as long as I can remember. And the amount of horse owners in the

world shows that I'm not alone in my deep love for all things equine.

In my later, early-adult years, my platinum-blonde Arabian mare Shekhan Schezar, or Shazzy-Bear as she became known, would flick and toss her super-long mane and lift her tail up high in the air, galloping like crazy while dragging a white flag on a pole. She was a prancing princess, but safe. Kind and protective of my children, she taught three of my daughters to ride and turned her neck to save them if it looked as if they might be on the point of falling off. Super clever and a real diva!

I also had Rumak, an Egyptian Arabian – a baby that I purchased when he was aged two – and started working with him as a potential show horse. He had the breeding and the poise, snorting as he went along. Later, I realised that he wasn't going to mature into the type of stallion that had the presence and stature to win against stallions of the same age. However, he seemed a better learner after he was gelded. He fretted when I wasn't with him, looking for my truck and following me in a trot with his tail up along the fence as I drove down the long lane, then nickering (giving a soft breathy whinny) as he watched me get out of the car. Sadly, he developed a major liver condition and, after just one showing at national level, he was found dead in his stall where he was boarded while I was away at the coast taking a short break. I was devastated. In shock. I had to get back home to find a suitable place for him to be laid to rest. The yard had video filmed finding him, so that I could give it to the vet when they did the postmortem. So tragic. After the verdict I decided that, if possible, he would be

cremated or go back to nature. I asked the vet to take a long piece of his tail as a keepsake to make a bracelet from.

I didn't buy another horse for a while, as I was reeling with the pain of losing my little boy. Grief stricken, I would lose time while working, as my mind would wander and relive happier days when I was riding and teaching my young stallion.

Before I was able to look for a horse of my own, I had to find out if I was ever going to be able to ride.

I did some research and found that the nearest Equine Assisted Therapy barn to me was in March, in the county of Cambridgeshire, a private yard, and it was run by a renowned Western horse trainer and rider called Andrew Fox.

I had decided on Andrew Fox as he had undertaken the difficult case of a man who had broken many parts of his body, including his shoulder blade and collarbone (on the same side), as well as the upper and lower parts of his arm, all on the same side too.

After I dialled the number for the barn, a sweet-sounding young woman answered. It was Andrew's wife, Rachel Fox, and my trainer and life-coach to be.

So I explained my situation and the background and where I had heard about Andrew's successful rehabilitation record. Rachel mentioned that he was very focused on the show circuit in the UK and had a few rides as a paid jockey in the USA. She said Andrew was aiming to produce a string of reining stars for his clients, that he only worked with one person on rehabilitation at a time and that he

would evaluate truthfully the possibilities for me, and if he felt I would be able to ride again and, if so, at what level.

I wanted to cry. What if he said I wouldn't be able to ride or I wouldn't cope with riding against able-bodied riders? There were no classes for disabled riders in the Western class. Breathing heavily, I asked if I could call back once she had spoken to Andrew and then decide on the next steps. We ended the call on that note.

The funniest thing was that I felt I had my foot in the door with Rachel. I instinctively knew that she would fight my corner so that Andrew would accept me as a client. I could wangle the rest during our first meeting evaluation tests. The first step was simply to get Andrew to agree to take me on!

I called back at 9pm to hear good news – Andrew had agreed to take me on! I was to call in the morning to schedule my sessions. When I put the phone down, I cried tears of joy.

The next day, I talked to Rachel again and booked a set of riding and health-evaluation sessions. This was to be a 15-minute overview where I would show Andrew my medical file, X-ray plates and prescriptions, with a 10-minute ride if possible. There was also a 15-minute cool-down period with the chance to have a cup of tea and a wash-up.

The review sessions also looked at any experience or emotions that occurred more than once during a session, and again in subsequent sessions. In notes, together we would determine actions and practice, or questions for my GP – anything that might be needed to get more out of the

sessions and get closer to my end goal. I also used that time to take vital medication and to eat plenty of chocolate, as I faced a three-hour drive home afterwards. It was a 178-mile round trip to the barn. If anything, I was dedicated!

As Andrew Fox, with his wife Rachel plus two kiddies, had decided to go back to America to take a job with 888Darling Ranch, it meant that I would need to finish my training within a few months. Before they left the country in 2008, they helped me to find my horse Bareley Whizable, the champagne palomino I had owned before Tommy Girl. It was decided that we should get the horse before they moved to the US so that I would have a few months of their training to help me get used to my new mount. After they left, I I found another trainer recommended by Andrew so that I could continue my rehabilitation.

My Restless Leg Syndrome (RLS) shows itself with an uncontrollable urge. I have to move my legs – it's part of my neurological issues. The symptoms can appear in the daytime but, more often than not, the RLS usually strikes worst when I am lying in bed at night. I start to feel an odd burning sensation in my legs (my left being worse than my right) and then tingling, aching and itching. Sometimes I feel like there is a bug crawling deep beneath the skin of my legs from just below my knees. From night to night the symptoms vary in intensity and duration. Rubbing my legs helps a bit but moving seems to make it more painful. Sometimes doing so even makes me yelp or scream. Riding provided a way of easing the general discomfort and, over time, the routine pains decreased.

My dedication to horses had been very obvious through all of my life. I had broken relationships with lovers and friends if they didn't understand or even try to understand the feeling and place of importance horses have in my heart and soul.

Tina always had an affinity with the horses in my life. Initially, as mentioned earlier, Tina was terrified of horses, recalling the pain of having taken a fall off a stroppy palomino Welsh section D mare when she was very young. This was while she was sharing a hack with her favourite Uncle Phil, who had been assigned a gelding dark bay cob type who bolted for home at the first opportunity. The whole hack was an experience she wouldn't forget in a hurry.

Courageously, Tina rode again in early 2001. We were in Austria and her mount was a palomino gelding who was a little excitable. I was riding a cute little dun mare in front of Tina when her horse slid down the side of a ravine. It must have been truly terrifying for her but the palomino did manage to scrabble back to the road with Tina and they were both safe, which was very lucky considering what had just happened. Sadly, the experience did put Tina off riding for a long, long while and whenever I asked her to get back on a horse in a vain attempt to help her get her confidence back, she refused, saying she preferred to watch me instead.

Knowing the level of attachment and affinity there was between me and my horse, Tina always made sure that she had the time and energy necessary to spend with me at the yard. The horses loved her too, nuzzling and nickering

when they saw her in a special greeting. Most of the time they would undertake mutual grooming as if they knew that this person is special to my owner, therefore she is special to me too.

I think that Tina knew that I would not give up riding and she often spent time with me at the barn. Indeed, she had a great job and was able to help fund a lot of the expenses involved with having horses. I had often said to her that, if I couldn't ride and be with horses, what was the point in living at all? But even though she understood my affinity to my four-legged friends, she couldn't help but show her concern.

'Are you sure you want to go and have rehabilitation riding lessons?' she asked before my first session. 'What happens if you fall off?' She added: 'You need to take a chocolate bar with you in case your blood sugar is low – you're going to be exercising so you'll need it. Or I'll get you some sweets for the journey, OK? Don't forget.' She was always taking care of me!

The sugar problem was yet another health issue. I feel nauseous and faint, and get headaches if I exert myself too much. After that, I feel exceptionally tired. I've had these issues for most of my life but never realised that they were due to my sugar levels.

'Promise me that you will call from the yard before you get on that horse, and when you get off, or ask Andrew's wife to call or send me a text to say everything is OK – promise me, all right, honey?' said Tina. So I promised. She knew I would never break that promise.

Before I started out on my ritual three-hour early-morning drive to March in Cambridgeshire, I would take part of my medication. Upon arrival, I then had a cup of tea and took the rest of my meds and a couple of strong painkillers, so that I would keep the pain at bay for a few hours during my ride.

There was a spring show a year later (May 2007) at the Horse Creek Arena, Stags Holt, March, near Ely, Cambridgeshire. Andrew and his wife Rachel took part in this. She was well placed and came in the top ten, and the first place was taken by Andrew.

My first ride was on PeeWee, a bright-dun Quarter-horse gelding. He was a stocky chap, just making 15hh, with a black mane and tail and with a visible dorsal stripe down his back. He was safe, honest and trustworthy with kind eyes and floppy ears. He had well developed muscles and great hindquarters. In fact, PeeWee was a fantastic horse all round. He was known in the show circles and his owner had heard of my situation and given Andrew permission to use him, as he had the perfect temperament to help me gain confidence – how right he was. PeeWee was a super-fast reining boy with great movement and the most wonderfully gentle nature. He had been voice-command trained to a point of being a 'push-button' horse. He was tuned up and ready for the show ring. If I'd had the money, as he was for sale, I would have bought him. Watching him in training when I arrived at the yard was very exciting. His spins would be a plus score and the circles were true circles and not oval shaped or 'square circles' either.

The first look that PeeWee gave me seemed to be one of

understanding. He put his head down towards the sand arena and lay low, showing a kind and gentle eye. Licking and chewing his bit, he was calm. If I was ever fearful, I showed him and he made me feel safe. I had found the 'inner matriarch mare', the old leader of the herd. I have proved to both myself and others that my 'self-preservation' skills are 100 per cent. I could get through the worst and come out the other side. My inner core was strong and felt indestructible, as many had tried to destroy me a few times; I had 'earned' my stripes, a place as the respected leader.

The gelding was aware of a secure boundary where personal space started and ended. He only once tried to push that boundary and my reaction had him recoil back to where he was meant to be – not in my face!

A group of people that were watching were more intent on keeping in tune with the goings on in the indoor arena. They fell silent watching PeeWee's reaction to me. It was clear that my strength energy and definite 'directional' attitude, although unseen by human eyes, was what the horse was reacting to. I wasn't thinking aggressively. I had just thought about what I wanted and that I had the authority, taking back my 'power'. I was forging ahead.

I wanted PeeWee to make friends and to be my friend. I rubbed his bent head and moved his forelock. Then, I walked away giving him time to think, to lick and chew. He watched me. I turned my back to speak to the people watching from the side of the arena. I became aware of a nose and hot breath from nostrils, a head placed carefully in the small of my back. PeeWee had calmly positioned his

head in my back. In his own way, he had come over to join me, I think he wanted to be my friend too. In that instant we understood each other.

Then I was ready to mount up. Rachel brought my pain-control medication across and a glass of water. I gulped them down. The mounting steps were brought across and I stood on the top step, then Andrew helped me into the wide Western reining saddle. Already aching, I slowly bent down and adjusted my bottom into the saddle. I had promised that I would wear a British hard hat and that was perched on my head. I wore my faithful old Tony Lama boots, just in case my legs or feet were to swell. They were made of lizard skin, so I would be able to stretch them a bit to get my feet out.

PeeWee was quiet and waited patiently. Andrew checked my stirrups and adjusted the length. He joined a line onto the halter – he wasn't taking any chances.

Over the following sessions, I started to deal with my emotional baggage and there sure was a lot of it. Through my rehabilitation sessions, horses were able to make progress in my healing where doctors and clinical psychologists had failed.

CHAPTER THIRTEEN

POLICE AT OPERATION YEWTREE

It took me several years to come to terms with the childhood sexual abuse I suffered after the horrific and painful memories resurfaced as a result of my injuries suffered in the 7/7 bombings.

With the help of my Tommy, I had managed to allow myself to finally put the thoughts and memories to rest in a part of my brain where they would stay for weeks on end, only surfacing if I was having a really bad day or night. I had partially accepted that things do 'just happen'.

I gave myself permission to slow down and allow myself a degree of 'acceptance', even 'aliveness', to filter through my days after I chose to be part of the living.

But just when I thought it was all over – well, as much as anything like that possibly can ever be over – a sequence of events happened that led to me consider ending the life that I had.

Therefore I carried on living in blissful unawareness, my memories now buried too deep to surface, until October 2012, when Operation Yewtree was set up by the Metropolitan Police to investigate allegations of abuse regarding the once hugely popular British entertainer Jimmy Savile. He was a household name whom everyone knew and absolutely loved; the kind-hearted guy, who through his hit BBC TV show *Jim'll Fix It*, helped thou-sands of British kids see their dreams come true.

Savile was also very well thought of because of his work for charity, most notably with Stoke Mandeville Hospital and Leeds Royal Infirmary. He raised millions for both hospitals, where he was given more or less a free rein to visit patients, particularly the children.

He died in 2011 and he was mourned by millions. But, in October 2012, the news broke that the Metropolitan Police had opened up more than 400 lines of enquiry into allegations of alleged abuse at the hands of Savile and that more than 200 potential victims had been identified.

The investigation was in all the national newspapers because it was just so shocking. Women told police how he had sexually abused them numerous times and that he had met them through his TV show at the BBC headquarters in London, and also through his charity work. Many of them were just teenagers when they say he abused them and, in many cases, raped them. The abuse allegations scanned four decades, from 1959 until the late 1980s, and police deemed that the abuse had been on a national scale. By 19 December 2012, the total number of alleged victims was 589, of whom 450 alleged abuse by Savile.

It wasn't only Jimmy Savile who was named and shamed either. As the weeks went by, several other household names from the BBC were arrested and bailed on historic sex-abuse claims, including the former pop star and already convicted sex offender Paul Gadd, a.k.a. Gary Glitter. Other people, famous or otherwise, who were arrested as a result of the ongoing investigations were publicist Max Clifford (who has since been convicted and sentenced), a former BBC chauffeur David Smith (who committed suicide before he could stand trial) and a former BBC producer, Ted Beston, who was eventually told that he would not face any charges. It seemed that every other week a celebrity was arrested and they were generally high-profile public figures that everyone knows and loves, including Rolf Harris.

What about the balance of celebrities that were known to Peter and those whom I personally had seen and whose acts I had witnessed – what about them? Surely each of them, too, should be 'a person of interest'.

All the circumstances where I had overheard the 'steamers' or 'uncles' talking about famous people and comparing what each had seen, clinging to each other with their hidden code: they never grass a fellow paedophile up. No one tells all about anyone else, because that way they save their own arse. It's a closed group; an old boys' network.

Oh well, who cares about the childhood memories of middle-aged woman anyway? Who indeed? The outcome is bleak for women of a 'certain age', who can't provide exact dates, times and an address for the abuse or even for

the abusers. Other survivors' decisions to speak or not to speak will become their own battle. Personally, living with a time bomb within me, I needed and looked for an option to at least get out of the room before the bomb exploded. There is no reward for coming forward, no arrests, not even a caution. One thread should be enough to assist police in the pursuit of their investigations – the web of life is all interconnected after all.

I've done my 'civic duty' with conviction, coming from the right place and trying to help the path of justice being served. During my police statement, I experienced soul-piercing moments that brought many tears, which later I viewed as a gift.

When all this started to come out in the national newspapers in October 2012, I was completely floored: shocked to my core. Items shown on the news or written in the papers would trigger floods of memories for me. I had to overcome the barrier of fear that was so ingrained in me from years of grooming and abuse. My eyes were as big as moons when Savile's brother was mentioned.

'Oh my goodness,' I thought, 'I don't want to go through this again.' Once again I faced the sex shame of my past as the world I had struggled for so long to bury began to awake in front of my eyes again.

I began to retreat to my inner point of safety as survivor's guilt set in once more. I saw my reflection in mirrors and glass-fronted shops and when I looked at myself, I could not see an end to the pain I was feeling at that time.

Tina was away in Bangladesh at the time with her good

friend Janet, working with the underprivileged and giving her time freely to outreach clinics. They had spent hours repairing hearing aids and packing and storing audiological equipment over a period of two years, working by holding clinics on a Saturday, so that they had, between them, accumulated enough time and funds to make the trip worthwhile. Saving furiously, they had paid for their flights themselves; together they were working with a leading charity in Dhaka, with a sub-centre in Chittagong.

Between the two of them, they had taken in excess of 2,000 hearing aids, donated by the British NHS, in addition to a full, detailed letter to the charities and the Bangladesh government, as well as having written permission to have the aids. The letter further specified and that all the hearing aids and equipment would be in full working order, repaired, with batteries supplied, all in aid of the Bangladesh people. All of this equipment had been generously donated by the British National Health Service. The airline, Etihad, had agreed to the hundred extra kilograms to get the pallets to Bangladesh.

All in one moment I thought that I couldn't let on what was bubbling underneath the surface within me, when Tina was so preoccupied with her mission of mercy. Once again I kept the larger percentage of my inner feelings in, and didn't share them at all.

It was in the very early morning, before sunrise, on the day that Tina left for the airport, that Janet collected her, with all her luggage and equipment. Tina closed the front door softly: her personal adventure was starting. Hearing

her leave, I did wonder if I would ever see her again. Somehow, in an unexplained way, I feel that there is a hidden jewel in silence. In that continued process, there is a beauty in keeping that silence in the future. I looked into my inner self, wondering, should I continue to maintain secrets throughout the following years?

By the time she was to reach Bangladesh and her hospital residence in the doctors' accommodation, my inner scars from inhumanity on many levels poured out, but not in a healthy dose.

There was trouble brewing.

Every night after dinner, Tina and I would chat online if the connection remained for long enough. Whenever we talked, part of me wanted to let out all that was happening inside me – the trauma, the shame, the memories that had been sparked by the latest news all over the television and newspapers – especially the latest revelation concerning Jimmy Savile's brother, Johnny. I was struggling to keep my emotions in but I didn't want to upset Tina or cause her alarm.

Only once did I brought up the subject that was causing me so much grief. 'Crikey, did you get news that there's been a further arrest with Savile and that the coppers have unravelled a similar situation with his brother Johnny?' I said.

But Bangladesh didn't follow the same news as the UK did and the opportunity for Tina to watch the BBC news at the time was unlikely. So Tina found it a bit odd when I blurted out my take on the exposé of Johnny Savile.

I left it at that – it was my attempt to open a line of

discussion and it had failed miserably. I closed up, retreating with my shame, trying to make sense of the senseless.

Tina had arranged with her mum to come to stay with me for a few days while she was away. Together we painted the dining room and the wall cupboards, which had been built by a local carpenter. I began to decorate the kitchen walls with plain white tiles to create a light and airy feeling. My idea was to change the colour of the cupboards from cappuccino to white. I was pushing myself really hard to keep my feelings and revelations secret, and to concentrate on the DIY projects that were to form part of the surprise I planned for Tina on her return.

One evening after eating dinner with Tina's mum, I spoke out and told her about some of my childhood. Although it felt good to get some things out in the open again, I felt shackled to the past and fatigue set in.

Less than a month after Tina had returned from Bangladesh, there was a knock at the door in the early morning. Tina had already left for the hospital and was due to pick up a colleague along the way. I thought it might be her colleague knocking, as sometimes she needed to collect items that Tina had forgotten to take with her for her job.

But it wasn't her. It was a very rude man, who looked like a gangster. He asked me about a council-tax bill I had forgotten to pay some seven years previously, just after the 7/7 incident. We had moved since then and

it was forgotten, falling through the cracks of our lives. It happens.

The pale-faced, shaven-headed man said that he acted directly for, and on behalf of, the County Council. He demanded immediate payment, in cash, saying that the council were aware of his call and that he had a mandate with the authorities to do so. He became aggressive – quite threatening – trying to place his foot between the front door and its frame. I was angry anyway. I stared at him and told him to remove his foot and wait outside. He stood outside my door, pacing like a wild animal expecting his prey to give in at any moment. He waited until I was able to make arrangements to pay, not in cash but by credit card. One phone call and it was sorted, with monthly payments made thereafter.

The violent streak of the County Council Collections representative was enough to push me over the edge. After I closed the door, I collapsed on the floor, sobbing. I leaned with my back against the front door, then fell forwards and curled up into a ball. The dogs were pushing their noses into my face, licking my tears and becoming agitated.

I felt like I couldn't continue with the pain – emotional or physical. I asked myself, did I even want to go on?

In that moment, in early November 2012, I thought about suicide.

My old 4x4 would serve the purpose. I would attach the garden hose to the back exhaust pipe and pull it into the car from the side nearest the front door so no one could see it from the road. I was going to write letters to each person, which I would seal in envelopes and leave in my room on

my pillow. I had already labelled my personal effects – jewellery and the like – to say who was getting what.

Getting up, I realised the dogs needed fresh drinking water and put two extra bowls down for them as well as two plates of extra food. I checked my chickens and did the same for them, with each receiving a bonus feed of laying pellets and birdseed with some grit for good measure, along with fresh water and wood shavings bedding. Even at that emotionally turbulent time, I remained concerned about my four-legged furry friends and my two-legged feathered companions. My will stipulated what was to happen with Tommy Girl, so I knew that was covered. Her barn fees were paid up, so there would be no issues there at all.

My choices were clear: leave the world with the secrets intact and avoid any further suffering, or stay alive and report what had happened and start on the road to healing from the child-sex abuse in the same way as I had from the 7/7 injuries. What a choice to be faced with! Not much to choose from – dammed if I did and dammed if I didn't, just in different ways.

I couldn't make my mind up as the day went on, despite how clear cut things had seemed to me earlier. Once the chores were completed with the animals and birds, the situation didn't seem as desperate as it had been in the morning. I did try to call friends and family but the best I could do was to tell them that I loved them lots and that they shouldn't forget that. In a way, I felt it could have been the last time they spoke to me, and I wanted it to be a good call, not a general chit-chat type of conversation.

Then I called the charity line Samaritans and spoke to one of their counsellors for nearly two hours. She was very concerned and arranged to call me back later to check that I was all right and that, as I finally promised her, I had chosen to live, rather than the alternative.

I will never forget the moment that I decided, after the advice from Samaritans, and from Tina, that I would deal with my demons and, as part of the programme for recovery, report my personal experience and evidence to the police.

In my statement to the police, I told of my memories of the BBC. The officers didn't appear surprised at the time when I talked them through what had happened. I clarified the position with my memory and the facts around the head trauma bringing about the child-sex abuse and rape. I, too, was a victim of the BBC sex-abuse scandal, although, in my case, the abuse was linked to Johnny Savile, Jimmy Savile's older brother. They were five years apart and Johnny worked for a long time at Springfield Psychiatric Hospital in Tooting, South London.

Peter knew Johnny through their childhood in Yorkshire. I recall that they had similar links and knew the same sort of people but I'm not entirely sure of any direct connection other than that they knew each other through mutual friends and contacts. Peter was in awe of Johnny, mostly because of his famous brother.

Just like Peter, Johnny was perverted in the worst ways imaginable and he attended many of the paedophile parties that Peter arranged. In fact, Johnny and Peter both

organised these parties because they had different connections in different parts of the country. Shockingly, their network of parties was known throughout the whole of the United Kingdom and even beyond its borders.

I remember Johnny Savile. He was a run-of-the-mill sort of bloke with his hair a bit wild on some occasions but he wasn't memorable or special for the way he looked – he was ordinary; someone you wouldn't look twice at if you passed them in the street. I'd say he was one of those invisible sorts of people who you would never remember if you saw them once in your lifetime. I met him on many occasions and he always seemed to smell funny – you could smell him almost as soon as he entered the room. I could never put my finger on what that smell was, but I noticed he had a creepy energy about him, like he was always 'up to something'.

Unfortunately, as soon as he opened his mouth, you were made well aware that he was there. He was very proud of Jimmy, his famous sibling, and he was always dropping his name as if it was impressive. I suppose, to the paedophiles, in those days it was pretty amazing – Johnny Savile was a celebrity in their eyes, just for being associated with such a huge TV star that everyone in the country seemed to know and love.

Johnny had a lust for younger children – much younger children – and babies, and for children with disabilities who couldn't move easily to get away from him. He did unspeakable things to them while laughing, knowing that they couldn't fight him off. I called him the 'Shitter' after witnessing him at his most depraved and perverted.

We were at a party with a group of young teenagers – I think most were around 13 years old. Peter, ever the fixer, had managed to find a man who was having his custody weekend with his daughter and he had paid the father to have the child lay on the floor on a tarp-type piece of fabric. The sweet little girl was unable to get away as she didn't look like she was old enough to crawl – she just lay there on her back, still in nappies, chattering away to herself in innocent baby babble. She still had her bib on, which was covered in baby food and dribble, but she was quite happy to lie there and play with her toy keys and rattle.

As she lay on the floor, she wiggled her chubby legs up and down and squealed loudly – I remember thinking how cute she was. She was shouting, as if she was testing her little voice out to get her daddy's attention and that of whoever else was in the room. Her big blue eyes sparkled in the sunlight that shone through the window. My eyes narrowed and my heart sank as someone closed the curtains. Nobody – not one person – moved to stop them doing what they were about to do. As I watched, I prayed that, as this was a little baby girl who was lying there, this would be different. I couldn't begin to imagine that this group of men would touch her in the way they touched me all the time – I felt as if a baby should be sacred and left alone because she couldn't physically or mentally defend herself from these monsters.

In seconds, the group of men surrounded the baby and I saw something that I had never witnessed before. I was sat on an 'uncle's' lap as he played 'rumpty-dumpty' with me

on his knee and, in my mind, I begged someone to come and get this poor, defenceless, giggling child off the floor before someone did something hideous. I strained to see what was happening. I saw someone take the baby's clothes off so that she was lying there completely naked for everyone to see. Johnny Savile stood next to the baby and he had already taken off his trousers and his pants and had started to masturbate while looking at the baby. At that moment, I wondered how, if at all, the little baby was going to be able to be a 'good girl', as she was too small to undertake any of the activities usually expected by men of that type.

My breathing quickened because I was so afraid for the baby – she looked like a baby dolly lying there on the floor, like those dolls in a box in the toy store. I clutched the small silver cross around my neck like a talisman and began to rub it, and I pleaded with God to please come and rescue this child before anything happened to her. The thought of her being raped or abused like I was by these vile excuses for human beings cut through me like a sharp knife. After what seemed like an age, while Savile stood over the baby, he then knelt down and began to touch the little girl's sacred private parts. She obviously had no idea what he was doing – he must have looked funny to her, as if he was doing a crazy dance to make her laugh. As he touched her, I knew that there was serious trouble coming and I panicked. My heart raced and I wanted to scream, to make a scene, to gain his attention and the attention of every pervert in the room. But I didn't dare because I knew that would mean a lot of trouble for

me, so I struggled to keep quiet while witnessing the horrors that were unfolding.

What happened next I have never forgotten even to this day – it was the most horrific thing I thing I have ever seen. After defecating over the child's face, Savile let out a loud grunt and ejaculated over the baby.

Poor little soul. I felt a tear rolling down my face and I fought back a sob. Fucking bastard – I wished he was dead and, if I could have killed him right there and then, I would have. The father grabbed his baby in an awkward fashion – he scooped her up in his arms and made off to the bathroom to get her washed and cleaned up. To this day I still cannot believe a father would allow his child to be used in such an horrific manner – in a sense he was even more depraved than the others because he willingly let it happen to his little girl. When he later emerged, she was clean, dressed and sucking on a bottle of warm milk. She seemed to be over her ordeal, wrapped in a cosy blanket, and she peeped out with a sleepy face. I was stunned and, again, I prayed that she would never ever remember any of her ordeal and that she would never be used again by her father, by Johnny Savile, or by any man. Of course, I knew that was wishful thinking but I prayed nonetheless.

Savile also loved teenage virgins and it was up to Peter as a fixer to find them for him through his connections. Many of these poor young girls were runaways from home who had no one to take care of them, and they had nothing in this world to their name. Peter and his friends would find them by scouring the streets late at night or early in the morning, pretending to be 'good Samaritans' who cared.

They would offer the girls all sorts of bribes to go with them, from a few pounds to a hot meal and a roof over their heads, knowing that these down-and-outs were vulnerable and scared. They preyed on their emotions by getting their trust. I am sure that these runaways regarded Peter as their saviour when he came across them; their rescuer from their lives on the harsh streets of London and Plymouth. He really was such an amazing, charismatic actor, who could promise you the world, and you would believe him. I think that's why the girls went with him; because he promised them a better life. He told them that they could stay with him and his friends so that they didn't have to go back to their previous lives. I think Peter even gave them false job prospects to reel them in.

I didn't have a lot to do with these runaways but I do remember overhearing Peter on the phone a few times talking about them. There were a variety of safe places where Peter and his friends would place the girls, usually for a few days until negotiations were made to find them somewhere more permanent. I can only speculate but I think that the more permanent homes were overseen by Peter's perverts so that, once they were reeled in, they couldn't escape. I am guessing that perhaps they were drugged, so that they wouldn't even want to get away, and I know that Peter often threatened to call their parents and tell them what 'naughty' girls they had been once they had been used and abused by his friends and clients.

All of their food and travel expenses were paid for by the men who hired them from Peter. The cold, hard-core types paid one fee and they were allowed an afternoon or

evening with them. During that short time, they were allowed to do most things with the girls. Blow jobs were allowed, of course, and masturbation– or a 'tilly' as it was known in their circles. They were allowed one full-blown sexual encounter, either in the usual vaginal way or anal, and a lot of men liked to masturbate themselves between the girl's breasts if they were big enough, or even between their feet. If the one sexual experience wasn't enough, they could pay for more and any sexual act that involved urinating (golden showers) carried another fee. These girls were a major money-making operation for Peter and one that he kept going for years. It was no wonder Christine's house was like a little palace with its up-to-the minute furnishings – even the garden looked like it should have been on the latest *Home and Garden* magazine cover. Everything that she had was paid for not only by me but, mainly, by these poor, defenceless young women who set out from their homes to leave a nightmare behind, only to find themselves in the middle of an even worse one from which they possibly would never escape. It was tragic and I felt terrible for them because they no longer had a future.

It was through the Johnny Savile connection that Peter found yet another way to pimp me out – and that was within the BBC's own walls at Broadcasting House in London. Even after we left the country to live in South Africa, Peter stayed in touch with all his paedophile contacts, I'm guessing just in case we ever came back, so that he could start up his child-abuse business again in the UK. He also had contacts in different countries and he continued his vile ring of paedophiles all over the world.

When I was 15, we all came back to England from South Africa for one of Peter's business trips, although it was billed as a 'family' holiday and we were going to visit London, Germany and France while we were over. I don't know what it was for but it was the ideal opportunity for him to keep his connections sweet in the BBC. I remember one weekday when Christine and Tracy stayed in Plymouth with Sarah for the day. At night, Peter and I stayed with his mum in Alma Road, Plymouth. His brother John and his wife Pam also lived there and ran the old three-storey house as a bed-and-breakfast, as it was in a prime position on a main road. His mother had no income other than her deceased husband's limited pension and she needed the money just to make ends meet. It was sad for her but, with John and Pam, they ran a pretty successful business and they were happy to put us up while we were in Plymouth. I loved being back in the UK with Sarah – I had missed her so much and I thought that, as we were only over for a couple of weeks, there was no way Peter would take me to meet any more 'uncles'.

During the day, if we were not dragged out visiting relatives, we were in Stenlake Terrace, Plymouth with Sarah. From my bedroom, I could still hear the ever-so-familiar railway sounds at the back of the house and it reminded me of being a young child again and the times when I used to stay with her. I lay in the back bedroom with just my annuals for company, away from the rest of them, who were in the front room chatting and catching up on life. The mid-terraced home, with the front door on the right, was within walking distance from the River

Plymm, near the Laira Bridge road. From here, it was a short walk down Lucas Road onto the cobblestones under the archway that ran under the train line and then on and up to the park for access to Tothill Park. I was able to walk about free again, unlike being in South Africa, where danger was around every corner and our home was like a fortress.

How I wished that I could stay with Sarah and not go back with Peter and Christine to South Africa. Sarah and I made wonderful memories during that stay. As a special treat one day, she took me into Plymouth city centre, where she bought me a white candy-striped jacket and a pair of white trousers. I thought I was the bees knees – they were so trendy! On another day, we went to the beach and had an ice cream and, on another morning, we went to the park but it wouldn't have mattered where we had gone, I just wanted to spend quality time alone with Sarah. She was still the same nurturing, loving person she had always been and, when I left to go back, she put her arms around me and cried. 'I will miss you so much, my lover,' she said. 'Make sure you take care of yourself.'

One day – I know it was a weekday – Peter took me to one side. 'Beverli, you and I are going to be taking a special trip into London today,' he said. 'You are going to love being in London!' He seemed rather excited and a little agitated himself that morning, smoking a lot more than was normal, as if he couldn't wait to go.

'Why are we going?' I asked, not wanting to be away from Sarah for too long. It didn't bother me that Christine and Tracy had to stay home – I'd long given up on those

two ever playing a big part of my life. They were inseparable, two peas in a pod, and they could find no time in their days or their hearts for me. It still saddens me to think about how, when Tracy was born, I was pushed aside like a piece of rubbish, cast out on my own so that Peter could get me firmly in his evil clutches.

Peter gave me one of his fullest smiles. 'We are going to a very special place,' he said. 'But you have to be really well behaved, OK? Be a good girl for me again. Business first, as usual! Can you do that for me?' There it was again! As soon as he said 'business as usual', I knew that we were going to be meeting some of his friends and that could only mean one thing for me. I shuddered, pissed off that, even on a holiday visiting relatives, he couldn't stop the urge to make money out of me, the sick pig.

I was so angry but I knew that I had to be well behaved. Peter had long drummed it into me that, if I didn't do as he said, I would be in a lot of trouble, so it was easier and better for me if I just complied with everything. This time though there was something that I wanted out of the so-called nice trip.

'I will be good. Could we go to Trafalgar Square so I can feed the birds, like in Mary Poppins?' I asked. Peter grinned again and puffed on his cigarette.

'Of course, like in Mary Poppins,' he said. 'I'll get a bag of bird feed for you to give to the pigeons. We'll stop on the way to the surprise. I promise you will see the birds, all right?' Peter never made any promises to me, not ever, simply because he could never keep them. It wasn't in his nature to be honest and true to his word in a positive way

– well, not to me; maybe with others he might have been different. The only types of promises he did keep were those he made when he was making vile threats to get me to do something I didn't want to do, like giving a customer a blow job or lying still while someone had sex with me.

We left to catch the train to London's Paddington Station and I wore my candy-striped jacket, my favourite item of clothing. I tidied my then fashionably short-cropped hair and I put on a little mascara and lip gloss, as I always did when meeting Peter's friends. I thought this one must have been extremely important though, since we were going into London and he had to make much more effort than usual. On our way into London, he didn't talk a lot about where we were going but I could see from his expression that this wasn't the norm.

Feeding the birds in Trafalgar Square will stay with me for ever. Peter gave me the bag of feed and I stood in the middle of the square, arms outstretched like my favourite Disney character, Mary Poppins. The birds came to me and sat on my arms and shoulders and I had never felt happier, freer or more alive. I'd long dreamed about being like the children from the movie, who had a lovely house and beautiful clothes but, more importantly, parents who loved them deeply. The sun blazed down on me that day like a magnificent ball of fire as the birds flew to me for their food. How I wished that I could be a bird like them, free to go where I wanted to, free of Peter and my unhappy home life and completely free of the men who used and abused me all the time. If only my life were different and I was like other teenagers, whose only

worries were, in my mind, to get their homework done and handed in on time.

So I left Trafalgar Square on an emotional high and we took a taxi to the BBC headquarters on Wood Lane. It was just a short ride and, when we got there, I was in awe of the building. We were taken to the back via a tiny circular road and that's where we parked, next to a few metal steps leading into the building. We were ushered into the building through this back door, quickly, to avoid detection, I assumed. Once in, we were told by our BBC guide that there was an entrance that led to the *Blue Peter* garden, close to where we had come in, and that we would be allowed to visit it later. That was an exciting thought. I'd grown up with *Blue Peter* and one of my favourite parts of the show was the crafts-and-gardening section. The thought of seeing that garden in real life lifted my spirits and gave me an incentive to mentally get through whatever was going to happen that afternoon.

I remember that there were props everywhere and wires snaking around the floor leading to TV-show sets. Peter and I carefully picked our way through the mess, so that we didn't disturb anything and gain attention that we were in the building, because I knew that we weren't supposed to be in there. There was so much to see; it was like being in a sweet-shop of sights and scenes I had never seen before in my life. People were rushing around with clipboards in their hands and costumes, all shouting loudly. It seemed like organised chaos and I felt very small right then. No one paid the slightest bit of attention to us as we picked our way through the corridors. It seemed that Peter was

known to quite a few people because several people stopped what they were doing and nodded their heads to say hello. The women, especially, smiled in his direction when they saw him. He had the look of a film star and that, along with his charm and wit, was enough to attract most women to him.

And I don't think that the staff who didn't recognise Peter had any idea why we were there. The suited-and-booted person who had collected us from the back door was very friendly and Peter gave him a special look, reserved for those who were aware of the 'dial-a-child' service he provided. When we had entered the BBC studios, I had wondered whether I might be lucky enough to be an audience guest on 'Top of the Pops' after I had completed my work, whatever that was going to be. As we walked down the long corridors, I could see by the way he looked around and by his brisk walk that we were looking for one dressing room in particular, and that we had to get there quickly before anyone asked any questions. The floors were sparkling clean and the corridors were modern and quite airy. I imagined that, when everyone had gone home, it would be a bit eerie. I focused on where we were going, as we were walking quickly. The dressing-room passages were all alike. You couldn't tell one from another and it was like we had entered a rabbit warren of rooms with bright lights over the tops of the doors. We went past what looked like a school blackboard, where the names of the producer and other people working on the show were written.

We were led to a dressing room and the person who had taken us there knocked on the door and opened it, so Peter

led me in. Inside was a youngish man in his thirties with a mullet (hairstyle with short hair at front and sides, but left long at the back), wearing lots of brightly coloured make-up and with a white towel tucked around his neck to stop him from getting make-up on his fancy clothes. I got the impression that Peter and this man didn't know each other on a personal level because very little was said, except when the stranger gave Peter a small handful of money. Peter went outside the door to keep watch and it was agreed that, after he had smoked a couple of cigarettes, he would knock on the door again and I would be released back to his care. His knocking on the door was basically a signal for things that were happening in the room to end. I knew then that I would have to do my best – same shit but a different day – to give this person a good time.

I could have screamed out and I was crying inside as I stayed behind with the man. He moved towards me slowly. 'My name is Paul. You can call me "Daddy",' he said in a low voice, to be sure that nobody heard anything at all. He picked me up and placed me in front of the big mirror area, quite gently and carefully, as if I were a prized porcelain doll. Then he pulled my panties aside and checked to feel that all was well in the small areas that should have been no-man's-land. I could tell he just wanted to get it over with because he didn't bother trying to kiss me or arouse me in any way. He opened up my jacket, looking for my newly formed breasts. Then quick and fast, he pulled his trousers down and I saw his inadequate manhood ready to penetrate. He found his marker and, as he raped me, I caught him smelling his filthy fingers – I guess, like many

other men I had had the misfortune of meeting, he found the smell a massive turn-on.

As I sat there, I started to count, as I usually did – it helped me to focus on anything but the unpleasantness of what was happening. I looked at the ceiling and thought, 'Get on with it, for God's sake.' Peter had told me that, when someone was about to orgasm – or in order to hurry them up – I should say in the cutest, most childish voice I could, 'Oh, Daddy, cum for me.' So as a dutifully 'good girl' I said just that and, as predicted, he had his orgasm straight away. He smiled at me, pulled out, hoisted up his trousers and went back to the mirror to check on his appearance.

There was a knock on the door and I thought it was Peter. However, it was a lady with a clipboard. 'Five minutes!' she said loudly, so I guessed that he was due on whatever TV set he belonged to.

Then there was another knock on the door and this time it was Peter. 'See you again,' he said knowingly to the man, and we were led back out of the building and into a waiting taxi. I never did get to see the *Blue Peter* garden, nor did I get to appear in the audience on *Top of the Pops*. I was brought back to the BBC another two times and I was raped again by two different men – I have no idea who they were, only that they were probably in their thirties and that they were possibly major TV stars of the era. I have no doubt that certain people within the BBC knew all about this practice of bringing in underage girls for sex with their TV stars and they let it happen, which is inexcusable.

After news of the Jimmy Savile sexual-abuse scandal was made public, I fell into a deep depression, as I was forced to remember those BBC rapes and the Johnny Savile horrors. Tina was at her wit's end with me because I was having nightmares every single time I shut my eyes and they were enough to wake me up screaming, as if I was being murdered in my sleep. We decided that the only way to deal with what I was feeling was to talk about it and that, by doing so, I might be able to help someone else who had been a victim of the BBC scandal. I spoke with my doctor and I was prescribed tablets to help me to calm down and think more clearly. They definitely helped me and that small amount of intervention, along with my conversation with the girl at Samaritans, was enough to give me the mind-set to call the police and tell them everything I knew about Johnny Savile and underage sex at the BBC.

It was a tough decision for me to talk to the police because I knew that the repercussions could potentially be very harmful. I did worry that no one would believe me because it was so long ago and my memories were sketchy at best but I felt in my heart that, the more of us who came forward to tell our personal stories, the more chance there was that justice could be served, no matter how many years ago the crimes had happened.

One of the issues I had recalled was abuse undertaken by a priest, who enjoyed both boys and girls. In later years, I saw letters that the priest had shown to Peter, where the head of the diocese had written to him with complaints and

allegations. Peter helped the priest cut down the 'noise' and silence the issues at a higher level. So basically, the priest got away with it.

Tina promised that she would back me all the way and we both knew that the road ahead wasn't going to be easy, as we knew that, the more I talked about it, the more painful would be the memories that would result. I know that Tina was concerned at first that, after everything else that had happened to me in recent years, I wouldn't have the strength to go through with it all. But I soon assured her that I was at a time in my life when, if me saying something publicly could persuade other victims to come forward and seek justice, it was worth it to me. I also felt that, by raising awareness of this horrific subject, somehow my story might touch other girls who are living the sexual abuse now and show them that there is an escape route and that there are people who can help.

I had planned to go to my local police station in Ashford, Kent to give a full statement but my close friend Councillor Richard Barnes, former Deputy Mayor of London, told me that he thought it might be better for police officers directly involved in Operation Yewtree to come to get the statements, as they were completely familiar with the case. I think he was worried about me having to give the same statement twice and how that would be more of an ordeal for me. I agreed and, within 24 hours, the lead detective from Operation Yewtree had called me and, after a long chat, we agreed that he could send his detectives to get a full, taped statement from me.

The Serious Organised Crime Agency (SOCA) was

already dealing with all the victims that had come forward after going public with the Jimmy Savile case and my testimony fell into the third category, 'Savile and Others', as I had not had direct contact with Jimmy Savile himself – but I knew his brother Johnny very well. The chief assigned two women, initially, as the detectives who took the taped evidence from me. Tina was asked to provide her statement to an officer in a separate room and sign it later, based on what she had answered when questioned.

The methods used by the detectives reminded me of the questions from the counter-terrorist squad that I answered after 7/7. It was more like an interrogation of me than it was an understanding towards me as a victim, and I had to go over my story time and time again, which was stressful, to say the least. Yet, as I remembered the abuse, I became hopeful that the parts of my life that were still lost in my mind would come back to me, to make me whole again, no matter how horrible it made me feel.

As I write, the new emotional turmoil continues and the issues come forward on a daily basis, especially when the SOCA detectives come over and do their further interviews and record statements, later bringing a typed version for me to sign.

I don't know whether, in the end, my statement will assist the police in making an arrest or not. Looking at it in the worst way, at least I've done my duty. I do pray that the endless hours of police interrogation will help my recovery, rather than set me back years.

When the Jimmy Savile case came to light, I was in a good place in my life and I had come to terms with the

bombings and the sexual abuse that I had suffered at the hands of Peter.

I started to write down all I could recall in a PowerPoint presentation – a good job we have advanced computers! As each flash, action replay and snippet of information flew into my mind, wherever I was I wrote it down, then typed it into the document later when I had the time. A funny thing memories – they seem to have a need to be triggered.

One of the detectives asked about Peter's death and roughly when he had passed away, but I couldn't really say with any accuracy, so they had to look for a death certificate. Peter had been very aggressive at the end of his life. Although impotent, he didn't stop trying to chase the young nurses in the medical ward. When they told him off, he attempted to throw one of them out of the window. Luckily for her, the windows had bars so, although she was hurt, she didn't learn to fly the hard way.

Christine had divorced him, as she had found out about his affairs, but I'm not sure whether she ever knew and had it confirmed about his paedophilia activities or his little gang. She never said.

The last time I went to see Peter, after a long break, I took my eldest daughter with me, when she was quite young. She has a similar look to me when I was her age. Peter looked at me and asked, 'Who are you then?' He didn't recognise me. I said, 'Beverli. I'm Beverli,' to which he replied, 'Rubbish! You're not Beverli. I don't know you. There's Beverli,' he said, pointing his bony finger aggressively towards my eldest daughter.

He had no concept of time. He was in hospital but

thought he was in a hotel. So that day, he told me to go away, as he swore blind he didn't know me at all. I took one last photograph of him and then we drove home. That was the last time I saw him alive.

Peter had left an estate but I refused to take money from him, as it would have been yet another 'payment' in lieu of what he did to me. It was almost like the bastard was trying to continue his control from beyond the grave. No chance – I am older, wiser and far more grumpy than ever I was. There wasn't a lot left of anything anyway – I think he had about 2,000 pounds in his estate. He had once lived a very good life and had always been financially very secure, but most of his money had gone on nursing home costs and his care before he died.

I signed over the money, my portion of the estate after legal expenses, to be divided between my four children and to be paid directly to them, and they received this in 2013 – I gave them 100 pounds each. Although it was only a small amount each, it was enough to buy something nice for them and have a day out, so it turned negative money into something positive. At the time, I had sleepless nights and days when I didn't want to get up because I couldn't stop thinking about it all again.

The thing that keeps me going is the deep belief that, by doing this, I am going to help someone along the way and, even if it's just one young girl, that's worth it.

Through their lawyers, the BBC have stated that they won't pay compensation to individuals through a caveat the individual has to be an employee of the BBC, otherwise there is no case, and they take no responsibility for what

happened on their premises at all. The details will all come out, piece by piece, when the very public enquiry goes ahead in England – and I will be watching, just like everyone else in the UK, knowing that my experiences have made a difference in making these people pay. Maybe then I can start to get my own closure.

CHAPTER FOURTEEN

ALL THE QUEEN'S HORSES

After I bought Tommy Girl and she settled into life in the green pastures of England, my riding abilities improved, as I was able to ride her four times a week and I was also able to 'long-line' her for a day a week. Long-lining is when a rider walks next to the horse with extra-long, more elasticated reins and, that way, without being on the horse, the rider can concentrate on bending the animal, and trying out new movements. It's good for the horse too because it's often easier to try new moves for the first time without the weight of the rider on its back. I was using her for free sessions for people with trauma issues as a 'taster session', so that the message about horse therapy would get out and get riders talking. I knew that she would be an enormous asset when it came to the horse therapy because of her beautifully calm temperament.

The joy I felt when I went to the barn to see her was

enough to leave me on a high all day. I became more positive, confident in not only my riding but my future. I guess you could say that she put the spring in my step again.

As soon as I drove up the sand road that led to the stable, she would run along the fence and, as I pulled up outside the stable doors, she would whinny to me, as if to say, 'Hello, Mum.' I loved that feeling – it was the best feeling in the world! Just knowing that, not only did I need her to make my life complete but that she also needed me to love and to take care of her, so we were equals, in a sense.

As with all horse relationships, it was – and still is – very much a two-way street, where the benefits for Tommy and me are huge. Throughout my horsey life, I can't even begin to make a mental note of the amount of help that they have given me on a daily basis in life, and I feel that I have coped with much more than I might have done without their intervention. The honesty and patience of horses brings out the best in me and, over the years, I was saved from my demons by horses. During the times when I was a danger to myself because of the dark thoughts I was processing, the love of a horse brought me back from the brink in the unique way that only that kind of love can.

When I started the horse therapy, my main goal was, of course, to conquer my balance issues and to be able to ride again properly, and unaided, as I had always done before. In the back of my mind, I did have another ambition, which at the time seemed absolutely crazy because it would never happen but it was one that, nonetheless, stuck in a

dark area of my brain, waiting to resurface when the time was right.

This huge goal was to be able to compete in a Western competition on a horse. I had competed before in England in Western riding on Three Times My Lady and Barely Whizable and also in South Africa, winning a number of national titles with a red-chestnut-coloured mare, Alpha Toby's Ximini, a further tri-coloured gelding, Alpha Toby's Fiddlesticks, and my loud black-and-white Appaloosa Quarter-horse stallion Cody, who won the national Halter classes at both the Vaal Show and the Rand Easter Show, which takes place each year at the national show grounds on the outskirts of Johannesburg. Shows, the preparation and the atmosphere were an exciting part of my life – events that I had loved to do.

Even before Tommy Girl arrived in the country, I had entered her into a big national show. I know it sounds like an awful lot to take on but failure didn't even cross my mind. It felt like the right thing to do and, although I was really pushing the limits of my recovery, I had to do it. My primary path with Tommy was to heal and regain my strength, confidence and the 'me' that I had lost not once but twice. I had lost the real 'me', as I never had a real childhood, and I had also lost the real 'me' when I was deep in a tunnel under the city of London on 7/7.

There was a huge leap of faith in those that knew Tommy well in Canada, that she was the right mare for me. I had an inner, almost instinctive knowledge, that Tommy would connect with me as much as I had already connected with her. From the moment I saw her and her owner Alexia

working with each other in their sand arena in their home thousands of miles away, I was swept away with sacred, simple and sure love for this animal. Those moments in time are etched in my mind for ever and see me through the darkest nights.

Alexia had said that Tommy always tried so hard to please and do whatever was asked of her, no matter how complicated, and she trusted her rider and handlers totally. She had told me that Tommy loved to be working and learning and that she enjoyed a challenge more than other horses. I could hear In Alexia's voice that she was going through something herself but dared not ask her about it. She told me that she relied on Tommy to give of herself and that she never disappointed her. If Alexia was feeling sad, she was a shoulder to cry on and she instinctively knew how to pick up her spirits so, with all this information in mind, I knew that Tommy Girl was the one for me.

In my mind's eye, I saw us together as a team, building a bond to get rid of all the fear and sadness in my heart, my soul and my mind. There was also another reason why I wanted Tommy more than anything – she was a survivor, just like me. When she was just 18 months old, she was running in the mountains with her mother when she had a terrible accident that almost ripped off her hind leg. No one knew what really happened; only that she managed to limp home slowly to the barn for help and it was only a quick-thinking vet and emergency surgery that saved her leg.

Her own path to recovery was long and she was nursed day and night by the Hazeldene family, who owned her.

They took it in turns to keep the wound clean, to hand-feed her, to give her medicines on time and just to be there for her because she was alone. She'd lost her young innocence that day – her playfulness – and for a while, they didn't know whether she would come back to them.

The family showered the filly with so much love that they became her saviours – they still say that it's almost like, because they weren't going to give up on her, she wasn't going to give up either. Their hard work and advanced medicine paid off and she made a full recovery. In fact, the recovery was so amazing that she never walked with a limp and, over time, showed just a long, fur-covered scar. Tommy passed her vet checks with flying colours and, slowly, she was backed and the family started to take her to shows. To call it a miraculous recovery is an understatement. So in my mind, Tommy and I already had a bond before we'd even met – we were not going to meet our maker just yet, for a start! We both chose life and I knew that we would enjoy our challenges together as we had so much in common.

Unfortunately, because she had been bumped off her first flight because there wasn't enough space, and then didn't leave Canada until a week later, she arrived 11 days after she was supposed to have done, which meant that she was only going to have two weeks of training with me before the show. I had just 14 days to get her into shipshape condition for the show but I was secretly hoping – and praying –that her background in Pleasure and Trail classes at the shows she had been taken to by her previous owner in Canada would be enough to see us through if all else failed.

It was all nerve-racking for me but I was up to the challenge I had made for myself. Tommy Girl had a great show record – she was the three times World Congress Champion in Western Pleasure and Hunter Under Saddle. As I mentioned before, she was a Rolls-Royce to my Morris Minor level, so I aware that I had to up my game a bit! There was no doubt in my mind though that she would carry me for that first show and I knew that she was going to be a star. In the event, however, not in my wildest dreams did I imagine we would do so well.

Finally, show day arrived: the American Pleasure Star of London Championship. I had entered for Western Pleasure, Western Showmanship, Western Horsemanship and my weakness, the Western Trail classes. All classes were aligned to the Western Equestrian Society in the UK but not approved by the National Snaffle Bit Association, as the show organisers hadn't applied for affiliation approval in the USA. There was no monetary prize assigned but there was a decent trophy, with sashes and huge championship rosettes.

There were a variety of riders at different levels present, with a good mix of Quarter horses, Paints, and a Paint-Cob mix, both geldings and mares, so there was a lot of competition. To my amazement, we won the American Pleasure Star of London Championship and we also won the Sadie Trophy and the KCL Academic Cup. I couldn't have wished for anything better. Tommy was so perfect for me, as if she knew what I was going to ask her to do before I'd even given her the aids. For someone who not so long ago was afraid to get back on a horse, I had come a long way.

After the show and our amazing win, I really wanted to give something back to the future Western riders, who are a minority in Great Britain. Most people in the UK ride 'English' style, which I enjoyed when I was younger but, over the years, I became fascinated with the gentler art of Western riding. As a family, we decided to sponsor a few classes and purchased trophies and a perpetual trophy for three classes to make entries for the following year more attractive. I felt that I had been given a second chance at life through the horses and I wanted to help others to do the same. I wanted to share the knowledge that I had gained from my horse therapist, Andrew Fox, because I truly thought I could make a difference to people who had suffered traumas. It felt like my vocation and who better to work with the healing horses than someone who had been healed herself?

So I volunteered my services, and those of Tommy, to provide 'taster' sessions at the indoor arena of The Priory Home Farm Equestrian Centre in the village of Bilsingdon, Ashford, in Kent. The arena was large, with a separate seating area, tea- and coffee-making facilities, and a full music and lighting system.

David was one of the people that took up the offer of a few free sessions. I remember everything about our time together to this day. He was in his fifties and disabled, with movement in one finger only. He had a specially adapted motorised wheelchair, like the one that Christopher Reeves – or 'Superman' – used for so many years.

My new friend said that he had waited all his life for the opportunity to touch a horse, to be around them and to

ride one. I guess it was like a lifelong dream of his to have some sort of a relationship with a horse, and that dream was finally going to come true.

I remember the day that they first met and it was magical – something I will never forget. David was really emotional as Tommy put her head in his lap and sniffed his hands. He looked at her with such love and gratitude in his eyes and a smile through the tears that had started to fall down his cheeks. Tommy gently nuzzled his face, as if she was telling him it was OK. He asked his carer to move away and he whispered to me, 'I have one last dream, Beverli,' and I wonder if he had an inkling that his time on this earth was almost done. 'Is it possible for me to lead Tommy in my wheelchair if I put the chair in its upright position, so that I can see?' I know that he was wondering if it might spook her but I knew that it wouldn't.

'She'll be fine,' I said. 'Let's give it a go.'

I placed the lead rope into David's hand and I allowed some slack, enough to be taken up with the motorised chair. I wanted to keep Tommy right up by David's head if I could. His head was in a vice to keep it from dropping forward, so I wanted Tommy Girl to be in his close vision, so that he could see her at all times. This was David's life-changing moment and, as such, it was of major importance.

Then I clicked to Tommy and she looked my way, as if to say, 'OK, Mum, let's do this.' Then she breathed on David as he started to move the wheelchair across the arena. She followed him, so that she was by his side the whole time. If he stopped his wheelchair, she stopped right

away. If they went a little faster, she kept up with him at the speed he was going. Tommy never tried to pull away – she just stayed as close as she could to David and helped him to achieve his goal.

There were sobs of joy from the viewing gallery as David's carer and friends watched him achieve his lifelong dreams. There was a hush across the barn as time stood still for David and everyone else who was witness to that incredible moment. I still choke up when I watch the video of that day and the other videos that I taped of his sessions with Tommy. David died about a year later and, in the weeks prior to his death, he told me that he had made peace with his life and that it was Tommy who had brought him to that wonderful place. I was heartbroken when he died but thankful that, in his last months, he had been able to let go of all the anger and resentment I think he felt about being in a wheelchair, unable to do anything for himself. Tommy gave him a certain sense of freedom and I know that he was forever grateful to her for that.

During my time at The Priory Home Farm Equestrian Centre, I worked with other case studies. There was a young woman in her twenties who suffered with bulimia and severe confidence issues. However there was one case study that really touched my heart. This was a young girl, aged 10, who, for some reason, had depression. She had a difficult home environment and her grandmother took her for a try at therapy.

She was such a pretty girl – a bit shy and retiring – and she said very little to me. I often wondered what her home life was like because she reminded me of myself at that age

– quiet and closed in. I thought that maybe she lived with her grandmother because there was some family conflict, like a child-custody battle. She loved to ride though and her connection with Tommy was evident from the first time she sat on her back. I tried to get her to talk during our sessions but she wasn't interested at first – she told me that she had a stepfather but she wasn't happy to talk about her biological father. She told me that she wanted to be independent and be strong enough to do stuff on her own and, like me, she also had a lot of issues with her mother. The few rides she had with Tommy helped her to release a lot of her emotions and bring her out of herself. Being around Tommy Girl and riding her started her path to healing, there was no doubt about it. The sessions were the start of a quiet revolution for this sweet little girl. I spoke to her grandmother recently and she said that she had come along in leaps and bounds since the riding sessions. Her grandmother credits Tommy with putting her on the road to a more normal, stable life and she said that her granddaughter is now a teenager who has blossomed into a beautiful, confident young woman, who has developed her own flair for life and for clothing. She had become happy in her own company, something that she wasn't able to deal with before her time with Tommy.

It never ceased to amaze me when I saw the calming influence that the horses had on my clients. No matter what they were suffering from, they left our sessions a bit happier, a little more enthusiastic and, in some cases, smiling broadly and already planning their next ride. What joy I gained from seeing these, often subtle, changes in

people who traditional doctors had, in many cases, pumped full of medicines to control the symptoms, rather than attempted to get to the bottom of what was making them sad or angry. Riding the horses allowed these folk to feel in a much better place, if only for 10 minutes or half an hour. They would talk about what had been troubling them, probably because they felt much more relaxed and unthreatened being around the horses. I loved my work with a passion and I felt like the luckiest girl in the world – I got to work with horses and people and I got to ride my Tommy every day too. I couldn't have been happier.

But while I was happy with my lot, something did happen that completely blew me away while I was working with the healing horses. In 2011 the Paint Horse Association made us aware that the Jubilee were asking to review American-imported horses and American lines to include in the American slot of the pageant show for the Queen's Diamond Jubilee celebrations in London in June 2012. In order to be considered, each owner had to send off the breed pedigree of their horse, the mother's profile and a few photographs of the animal in tack and without tack, and also any pictures from shows.

I thought that I might enter Tommy's picture because, if she was chosen, it would be great publicity to highlight the beauty and grace of the American Paint. Tommy was very fit and I knew that she would manage easily with the noise of the crowds and the hustle and bustle of it all. In Canada, she had been filmed at different shows and she had also been at several World Congress Western horse shows, so she was well aware of the set-up. With all this experience

behind her, I didn't expect her to get excited or react badly, which made her an ideal candidate for consideration.

Next I sent Tommy's application file to the show director, who chose a few Quarter horses and two American Paints to be in the parade. My Tommy and a striking chestnut Overo mare were chosen to star in the Native American piece, which involved attacking a stagecoach to re-enact the Wild West! As Tommy is Western trained and she had experience of being in front of large crowds, she didn't need any training before the Queen's Jubilee. When I received the letter confirming that Tommy had been chosen, I screamed with excitement and sheer joy. I couldn't believe that out of all those applications we had been chosen – it seemed such a fitting thing for us to do, especially as the ceremony was to commemorate all that was great in Great Britain.

I had hired a proper horse lorry to take Tommy to Windsor Castle, her home for the weekend of the Diamond Jubilee. Tina and a friend, who had agreed to be Tommy's groom, came with me. As it was early on a Saturday morning, the roads to Windsor were quiet and, when we arrived at Windsor Castle, unable to hold back our excitement, we were ushered by marshals to the security entrance, where the appropriate searches and transport reviews were undertaken. Our passports and driving licenses were checked and we were assigned site permits and given our security tags and the data chip we required to be able to eat at the mess and dining hall. In true British style, it started to rain – and it didn't stop for most of the day!

At Windsor Castle the scene was colourful. There were horses and their owners everywhere and people were shouting, and horses neighing loudly to each other. It was rather like being at a huge show, with numerous first-aid tents for humans and horses, except this was a performance that was more important than any we had ever been to before. It was a privilege to even set foot in those majestic grounds and it was a little nerve-racking, although Tommy took everything in her stride, of course.

The castle was straight in front of us as we checked into the Snooze Box, which was to be our home while we were at the show. Once on the show grounds, it was very difficult to get back out again as security was tight – there were uniformed policemen in great numbers, and I am sure there were countless others in civilian clothes. The Union Jack was everywhere and I felt proud to be British. Looking back, the Union Jacks I'd seen reminded me of the red, white-and-blue jacket I had worn when I was at the BBC... and of the three rapes I'd suffered there too. The Union Jack was a major fashion theme at the time, a bit like hot-pants once were, and seeing all those Union Jacks did bring back memories. I refused to dwell on it – I wasn't going to let anything ruin that experience for me and, besides, there was so much to see and do to really take my mind off everything and all I had to do was to focus on the parade.

At the Windsor Show, the shops and stalls were like clubs for the posh folk, and for the stream of tourists that had come to see the parade and to celebrate with the Queen. The fact that I was there, not only witnessing the

glorious spectacle but also as a part of it – a child who had grown up used, abused and severely damaged – was really quite an accomplishment and, again, I felt a great sense of pride that I had made it through the major ups and downs of my life to see that day.

I was the child who had survived the dreadful 'Summer of Love' in 1967, being loved in the oddest of ways by older men who smelt of cigarette smoke; those that believed in free love and flower power and wearing kaftans. Thinking back, it was a strange time, with bells and flowers and everyone walking around holding two fingers up, saying, 'Peace, man,' none of which I understood at the time. Back then, all I needed was love, just like the song, but I got none. It was a time of drugs and swinging, which just meant that Peter made more money. The dynamism of the 2012 show was similar to the 'Summer of Love' and the happy-go-lucky way that everyone enjoyed themselves and got along back in those days. There was intense energy and excitement in the air, even after the rain and the muddy conditions that had marred the preparations slightly. As I walked around the grounds of Windsor, I did wonder what people would say if they knew my history. It wasn't exactly a typical English-rose background.

Whilst there I met the Regimental Corporal, Major Warren Brown, the Household Cavalry's senior soldier, who was originally from Canada, and he seemed to be running the show. He mentioned that all the soldiers had to learn the drills, commands and ceremonies, which I found really interesting. Major Brown was an interesting

character – he had a kind smile and he treated me like an equal. He asked about Tommy Girl and, as she had come to the UK from Canada, he seemed secretly proud that his countrymen had produced yet another fine horse to participate in the performances in front of the Queen of Great Britain.

We carried on walking through to the indoor temporary-barn marquee towards the side tent that had been erected for the cavalry to place all their extra gear; the additional equipment to the huge trunks that were placed outside each stable. There was a sentry hut, like a small shed, that was positioned next to the barn entrance, which had a sentry in it overnight. This was quite handy too as, if anything happened to our horses, the Major had arranged for the alarm to be raised.

The backstage areas were electric. We ran towards the stables and past the Canadian Mounties as they were hanging their tack up on spikes and feeding their horses. Tommy's late dinner was ready for her. She was very hungry, as were the rest of the horses in the American squad. I led her into her stable and took her tack off. After a quick shake, she was thirsty and played with her bucket of water before drinking. She seemed to wash her mouth out, spitting out water all over the pace. She loved the chaos and watched everyone and everything with what seemed like great interest.

We had rehearsals twice that day: at midday, then at 2pm. The main arena and show area were used each time. There was a small paddock that was used to get the horses warmed up by us before we handed them to the riders,

who were ready to go in and practice. Tommy was ridden by a real American Indian called 'Hawk That Flies First', although he went by his westernised name of 'Larry'. He was every inch an authentic American Indian and most of his beliefs had been passed down through generations. He had a small ranch in the USA, where he owned a number of horses himself. I had quite a few conversations with him about his strict breeding programme for his horses and the ways in which he respected the land he was given. In my opinion, he was a brilliant choice to ride Tommy, and as soon as the two started practising for the event together, I saw that they clicked. I had no doubt in my mind that my girl was going to make me proud.

The day itself dawned and we were told that tickets were going for £600 and on the black market and eBay for anything up to £1,000! That was crazy money but, when you thought about it, this was an event that was going to go down in history, never to be forgotten. And we were a part of it all – it didn't seem real. Tina had been assigned a ticket for the show and she took her place in the stands with me on the left-hand side of the Royal booth, which was where the families of participants stood. As participants, we had the option of either a navy-blue or black jacket with the official Jubilee insignia designed for the event. The jackets had the GB flag on the sleeve and that day I wore mine with pride. As I watched Tommy and Larry, my heart filled with such elation. This was truly the biggest honour of my life; a day that I don't think I will ever forget.

Early in 2013 I received a letter inviting me to No. 10

Downing Street to pick up a painting I had done that was hanging on the Prime Minister's walls and was seen by the visiting Olympic athletes and the Paralympic winners too. The 'Challenge' was an artwork I had painted from 2006 through till 2011 – through each PTSD-trauma episode, every nightmare, every attack of insomnia, the list goes on. The painting sessions were a further piece of the therapy jigsaw puzzle.

John Boy, a committee member of our Survivor's Coalition Foundation (pre-charity status), had approached the office of the Prime Minister, David Cameron, to ask if he would host the painting to be on show at No. 10, as it was such a poignant reminder of the terrorist bombings, something we shouldn't merely forget. There were still so many lessons to be learned from what had gone wrong on that fateful day, so we wanted to keep the memories as fresh in our government's mind as we could, so that investigations would continue.

After a lot of organising, the date was set for 12 April 2013. I was going to have to travel into London on my own, on public transport, which was always stressful for me, as I found myself looking everywhere and going into 'hyper-vigilant' mode. It was a monumental day for me. I was excited about going into the Prime Minister's home, but I was terrified about getting the train into London. I booked the tickets early so that I wouldn't have to wait in long queues and I decided to get the 11am train to St Pancras International, which would give me almost an hour to get a taxi across London. I wore a navy-blue lace dress with a tight pair of navy-blue pedal-pusher trousers

underneath. I pushed the trousers into my leather over-the-knee boots and I donned new jewellery that I had made. Even though I was as nervous as hell, I made the effort to look the part.

On the way to the train, I thought I was going to be sick several times. I was afraid to get into the carriage – it was that simple. I pushed fears about terrorists and bombs to the back of my mind and, instead, I concentrated on the good things in my life, like the horses and being honoured by this visit to London. Many tourists got on that train with me and, the more that got on, the more my heart raced and my palms became so clammy that I had to keep wiping them with a handkerchief. I started to sing in my head, no song in particular, over and over again, to block out what was going on around me.

And I made it. I got off the train onto platform 12 and I made my way through the crowds, resisting the urge to run. I caught the cab to Downing Street and, when I got there, all I could see were dozens of photographers and film cameramen who were there because of the death of Margaret Thatcher. They weren't for me, of course, and I slipped in through the door quietly after I had gone through security.

I remember standing at the front door of 10 Downing Street thinking how little it was: just one white stone step leading up to the plain brick frontage. The door was a bit on the narrow side for such a stately house and its six panels were made of black oak. It was surrounded by cream-coloured casing and prettied up with a semi-circular fanlight. There was a knocker in the shape of a lion's head

in the middle of the door. I banged on the door and it opened, to reveal a smiling face. This benign person let me and a good friend, John Baker, who runs The Survivors Coalition Foundation, in and there we were in the entrance hall – it was beautiful, with a shiny black-and-white chequered floor and a 'guard chair' in a dark cherry red in one corner to the right of a fireplace. I was in awe of the place.

The 'Challenge' painting was hanging on the wall by the side of the door along with other paintings that people had done. I saw my picture and I was as proud as punch. Although David Cameron wasn't there for the short ceremony, he had written a beautiful letter about my artwork. In the letter, he said that we should stamp out evil in all its forms. He also commented on how my work with the Survivor's Coalition Foundation showed what sort of a survivor I had become. He went on to add that the painting had been seen by the Olympic Team and other dignitaries.

Sometimes, in special cases, words are very comforting and, while they were being read out by one of Mr Cameron's aides, my eyes filled with tears. It was unusual for me to hear things being said in a positive and lovely way about me. I was a survivor in every sense of the word and I was proud. The journey to that point in my life had been long and difficult but I had made it, and I was standing in the Prime Minister's home, to top it all off!

I've had a pretty incredible couple of years and I've experienced happiness in a way I never thought I would. I'm at that stage in my life where, after all the heartache and unhappiness, I can breathe again. I can look around

the world and think that it's a pretty good place, really – I think that working with the horses, and especially having Tommy Girl, has restored my faith in mankind. It might sound dramatic but it's absolutely true. There have been times in my life when I have considered ending it all, especially when the Jimmy Savile scandal came to light, but it was Tommy who brought me back from the brink.

After everything that has happened in my life, after all the ups and downs, I have now found a sort of peace with Tommy and the other horses I work with regularly as part of the Equine Assisted Therapies group. I get so much peace not just from being around the horses but by being around the people they are helping. Knowing that the little girl who I just worked with can now manage a smile and a laugh, or the severely depressed young man who hated his life can now find a reason to go on after riding the therapy horses gives me so much joy and a reason to get up in the morning. I've known all my life that horses have the most amazing, healing effects on people – I doubt I would be here had it not been for all the horses I have been lucky enough to ride and to love. Horses will be forever be a part of my life and I believe that they will always give me the strength and the courage to carry on, no matter what else life throws at me.